Annual Update

2012

UK Government & Politics

Neil McNaughton

Paul Fairclough

Eric Magee

PHILIP ALLAN

Philip Allan Updates, an imprint of Hodder Education, an Hachette UK company, Market Place, Deddington, Oxfordshire OX15 0SE

Orders

Bookpoint Ltd, 130 Milton Park, Abingdon, Oxfordshire OX14 4SB
tel: 01235 827827
fax: 01235 400401
e-mail: education@bookpoint.co.uk

Lines are open 9.00 a.m.–5.00 p.m., Monday to Saturday, with a 24-hour message answering service. You can also order through the Philip Allan Updates website: www.philipallan.co.uk

ISBN 978-1-4441-6887-7

First published 2012
Impression number   5   4   3   2   1
Year   2016   2015   2014   2013   2012

Printed by the MPG Books Group

Hachette UK's policy is to use papers that are natural, renewable and recyclable products and made from wood grown in sustainable forests. The logging and manufacturing processes are expected to conform to the environmental regulations of the country of origin.

Contents

Chapter 1

2011 elections: who won, who lost and why?

Exam success

The up-to-date facts, examples and arguments in this chapter will help you to produce good-quality answers in your AS unit tests in the following areas of the specification:

Edexcel	AQA	OCR
Unit 1	**Unit 1**	**Unit 1**
Elections	Participation and voting behaviour	Participation and voting behaviour
	Electoral systems	Electoral systems

Context

Elections occurring in the year immediately following a general election rarely provide an accurate indication of the outcome of the next UK-wide poll. The tendency towards high levels of protest voting in such contests, however, can provide a useful snapshot of the degree to which the party or parties in government at Westminster have been successful in their efforts to seize the initiative and engage with the public at large.

In this context the five by-elections, the quadrennial elections to devolved legislatures in Scotland, Wales and Northern Ireland, and the various local government elections that took place in 2011 provide a measure of public opinion a year on from the 2010 general election.

This chapter gives an overview of the main elections that took place in 2011. In doing so, it answers the following questions:

- What elections took place in 2011?
- Who were the main 'winners' and 'losers' in each of these contests?
- Why did some parties fare better than others?
- Can we learn anything by studying the results in 'second order elections'?

What elections took place in 2011?

UK entry into the EEC (now the EU), the advent of devolution and the restructuring of local government that has occurred over the course of the last two decades have resulted in a situation where scarcely a year goes by without an election of note. By-elections to the Westminster Parliament — occurring periodically as a result of the death, retirement or resignation of an incumbent MP — add to this rich electoral tapestry.

2011 saw a number of significant electoral contests (see Table 1.1).

Table 1.1 2011 elections

Elections to devolved legislatures (5 May)
The Scottish Parliament
The National Assembly for Wales
The Northern Ireland Assembly
Local government elections (5 May)
England: 9000 seats were contested across 279 English local authorities
36 metropolitan borough councils saw one third of their members elected
49 unitary authorities saw elections: 29 saw all seats contested; 20 saw one third of seats contested
194 shire district councils saw elections: 127 saw all seats contested; 67 saw one third of seats contested
Directly elected mayors were chosen in Bedford, Leicester, Mansfield, Middlesbrough and Torbay
Northern Ireland: all seats were contested across 26 unitary authorities
Scotland and Wales: no local elections were scheduled

By-elections	
13 January 2011	Oldham East and Saddleworth
03 March 2011	Barnsley Central
05 May 2011	Leicester South
09 June 2011	Belfast West
30 June 2011	Inverclyde

Who were the main 'winners' and 'losers' in each of these contests?

Devolved bodies

The 2011 elections to the Welsh Assembly and Northern Ireland Assembly were far less noteworthy than those to the Scottish Parliament.

Wales witnessed a virtual repeat of the 2003 Assembly election, with Labour securing 30 of the 60 seats available — tantalisingly short of the number needed to exercise full single-party control (see Table 1.2). Back in 2003, Labour decided to 'go it alone', forming a single-party administration. Unsurprisingly, the party took the same road in the wake of the 2011 elections. The only other outcome of note in 2011 was that the proportion of female Members of the Welsh Assembly (MWAs) declined once more (just as it had done back in 2007). The gender balance that was once said to be one of the great success stories of devolution in the Principality is not, therefore, all that it once was.

Table 1.2 Elections to the National Assembly for Wales, 2007 and 2011

Totals (constituency + regional)	2007			2011		
	Votes	%	Seats	Votes	%	Seats
Conservative	427884	21.9	12 (5 + 7)	451162	23.8	14 (6 + 8)
Labour	603880	30.9	26 (24 + 2)	751612	39.6	30 (28 + 2)
Liberal Democrat	258910	13.3	6 (3 + 3)	176608	9.3	5 (1 + 4)
Plaid Cymru	423878	21.7	15 (7 + 8)	352706	18.6	11 (5 + 6)
Others	238326	12.2	1 (1 + 0)	166053	8.7	0

Gender of MWAs						
Men			32 (53%)			36 (60%)
Women			28 (47%)			24 (40%)

Source: adapted from Hawkins, O. (2011) *National Assembly for Wales Elections: 2011,* House of Commons Library Research Paper 11/40 (2011).

The 2011 Northern Ireland Assembly elections were similarly unremarkable. While those parties once seen as occupying the more extreme ends of the political spectrum in the province (the DUP and Sinn Fein) made minor gains at the expense of the more moderate SDLP and UUP, the elections did not result in a significant reordering of the Northern Ireland executive (which is required under law to operate as a coalition). The DUP took control of four ministries in the new executive, with Sinn Fein taking three, the Alliance taking one (in addition to the justice ministry) and the UUP and SDLP taking one-a-piece. Once again, the STV system employed in elections to the Assembly produced high levels of proportionality (see Table 1.3).

Table 1.3 Elections to the Northern Ireland Assembly, 2011

Party*	Seats (108)		First preference votes	
	Number (change)	%	Number	% (change)
Democratic Unionist Party	38 (+2)	35.2	198436	30.0 (–0.1)
Sinn Fein	29 (+1)	26.9	178222	26.9 (+0.8)
Social Democratic and Labour Party	14 (–2)	13.0	94286	14.2 (+1.0)
Ulster Unionist Party	16 (–2)	14.8	87531	13.2 (–1.7)
Alliance Party of Northern Ireland	8 (+1)	7.4	50875	7.7 (+2.5)
Traditional Unionist Voice	1 (+1)	0.9	16480	2.5 (+2.5)
Independent	1 (0)	0.9	15445	2.3 (0.0)
Green Party	1 (0)	0.9	6031	0.9 (–0.8)
Progressive Unionist Party	0 (–1)	0	1493	0.2 (–0.3)

* parties not winning seats in both 2007 and 2011 are excluded

Source: adapted from Cracknell, R. (2011) *Northern Ireland Assembly Elections: 2011,* House of Commons Library Research Paper 11/42.

It was in Scotland, however, that the 2011 elections were truly ground-breaking (see Table 1.4). Many commentators view the decision to adopt a hybrid Additional Member System in elections to the Scottish Parliament as a deliberate attempt on the part of those at Westminster to prevent a situation in which any single party (and, more specifically, the nationalist SNP) would be able to secure a working majority in the chamber. The fact that the SNP managed to do just that in 2011 not only afforded the party the opportunity to govern alone, but also gave it the means to advance its separatist agenda from a position of great strength. Crucially, majority control of the parliament raised the prospect of a nationwide referendum north of the border on the question of full independence. Should this vote, promised before 2015, deliver a decisive 'yes' vote, it would be morally and politically difficult for the Westminster Parliament to resist such calls, whatever the legal niceties.

Table 1.4 Elections to the Scottish Parliament compared, 2007 and 2011

Totals (constituency + regional)	2007			2011		
	Votes	%	Seats	Votes	%	Seats
Conservative	618 778	15.8	17 (4 + 13)	522 619	13.1	15 (3 + 12)
Labour	1 243 789	31.8	46 (37 + 9)	1 153 996	29.0	37 (15 + 22)
Liberal Democrat	556 883	14.3	16 (11 + 5)	261 166	6.6	5 (2 + 3)
Scottish National Party	1 297 838	33.2	47 (21 + 26)	1 779 336	44.7	69 (53 + 16)
Green	85 548	2.2	2 (0 + 2)	86 939	2.2	2 (0 + 2)
Others	104 713	2.7	1 (0 + 1)	176 102	4.4	1 (0 + 1)
Gender of MSPs						
Men			86 (67%)			84 (65%)
Women			43 (33%)			45 (35%)

Source: adapted from Sandford, M. (2011) *Scottish Parliament Elections: 2011*, House of Commons Research Library Research Paper 11/41.

Local government elections

It is not uncommon for the party (or parties) in government to face heavy losses at local elections. The Conservative Party found this to its cost between 1979 and 1997, and New Labour faced losses on a similar scale between 1997 and 2010.

Even in the normal course of events, voters inevitably regard such contests as an opportunity to register a protest vote — a chance to send a message to those in office at Westminster. Against the backdrop of the burgeoning economic crisis and the coalition's austerity programme, the potential for such protest was clearly heightened.

Box 1.1 The timing of local government elections

- In England, councillors are elected for 4-year terms under the first-past-the-post system.
- London borough councils, county councils and some other authorities are elected in their entirety every 4 years.
- Other authorities divide councillors into two or three cohorts, electing a different cohort at each election.
- Authorities where councillors are divided into thirds hold elections every year, with no elections calendared in those years that coincide with county council elections.
- Those authorities that divide councillors in halves elect half of their members every 2 years.

In this context, it was perhaps surprising that the Conservatives in fact polled a larger share of the popular vote than Labour at the May 2011 local elections, with the party making a net gain of 86 seats and ending the night in control of 157 councils (a net gain of three). Though the Labour Party was more successful in converting votes into seats (see Box 1.2), the result suggested that voters were not targeting their fire on the larger of the two parties in power.

This sense was reinforced by the fate of the Conservatives' coalition partners, the Liberal Democrats, who suffered a net loss of over 700 councillors and relinquished overall control of nine of their 13 councils.

Box 1.2   2011 local government election results

Conservative Party

- 38% of the popular vote
- a net gain of 86 seats
- won or retained control of 157 councils (a net gain of three)
- made 13 gains from no overall control (NOC): three from the Liberal Democrats, one from Labour and one from other

Labour Party

- 37% of the popular vote
- a net gain of 839 seats
- won or retained control of 58 councils (a net gain of 27)
- gained control of: Blackpool, Gedling, Gravesham and North Warwickshire from the Conservatives; Chesterfield, Kingston upon Hull, Newcastle upon Tyne from the Liberal Democrats; 21 councils from NOC

Liberal Democrats

- 16% of the popular vote
- a net loss of 748 seats
- won or retained control of ten councils (a net loss of nine)
- lost control of: Lewes, North Norfolk and Vale of White Horse to the Conservatives; Bristol, St. Albans and Stockport to NOC

Others

- the Greens won or retained 79 seats, thus holding more seats on Brighton and Hove council than any other party
- the British National Party retained just two seats, losing 11

Source: adapted from Tetteh, E. (2011) *Local Elections 2011*, House of Commons Research Library Research Paper 11/43.

Although attempts to extrapolate such results onto a bigger electoral canvas are fraught with problems, such widespread losses would certainly have given leading Lib Dems pause for thought, not least because the party has traditionally looked to build support nationally on the work and reputations of those Lib Dems elected to local government.

Mayoral contests

5 May 2011 saw the election of five directly elected mayors, in addition to the contests to fill the various local council seats contested on the same day. These mayoral contests took place under the Supplementary Vote (SV) system used in all such contests in England. Two of the candidates (Sir Peter Soulsby in Leicester and Ray Mallon in Middlesbrough) were elected without the need for any vote transference, having secured the required 50% on first

preferences alone (see Table 1.5). The contest in Torbay, which saw Nicholas Bye (the incumbent mayor) standing as an independent against Gordon Oliver (the official Conservative Party candidate), was far closer. Bye only trailed Oliver by 19% to 26% on first preference votes, though Oliver ultimately secured victory with 57.4% of the ballot, once votes had been transferred from eliminated candidates.

Table 1.5 Mayoral contests, 2011

Authority	Former mayor	Party	Mayor-elect	Party	% first pref
Bedford	Dave Hodgson	Lib Dem	Dave Hodgson	Lib Dem	38%
Leicester	N/A (new post)	N/A	Sir Peter Soulsby	Lab.	55%
Mansfield	Tony Eggington	Ind.	Tony Eggington	Ind.	38%
Middlesbrough	Ray Mallon	Ind.	Ray Mallon	Ind.	50%
Torbay	Nicholas Bye	Con.	Gordon Oliver	Con.	26%

Source: adapted from Tetteh, E. (2011) *Local Elections 2011*, House of Commons Library Research Paper 11/43.

By-elections

The four by-elections held in Britain in 2011 would certainly have given the two parties in office at Westminster food for thought (see Table 1.6). Though all four contests were held in seats where Labour might reasonably have been expected to win, the average swing in favour of the Labour Party (8.5%) and the average swings against both the Conservatives (7.7%) and the Liberal Democrats (7.1%) where perhaps surprising, given the relative fortunes of the main UK parties at the 2010 general election. While those in the Labour leadership team might have been alarmed by the SNP's advance in Inverclyde (coming as it did so soon after the nationalists' triumph at the Scottish Parliament elections), the bigger picture was more positive for a party widely seen as having lost its political mojo just a year before.

Table 1.6 By-elections to the Westminster Parliament in Britain, 2011*

Constituency		Outcome	Majority	Swing		
				%	From	To
13 January	Oldham East and Saddleworth	Labour hold	3558 (+3455)	11.95	Conservative	Labour
3 March	Barnsley Central	Labour hold	11771 (+678)	13.30	Lib Dem	Labour
5 May	Leicester South	Labour hold	12078 (+3270)	8.35	Lib Dem	Labour
30 June	Inverclyde	Labour hold	5838 (−8578)	8.85	Labour	SNP

*excludes the Belfast West by-election held on 9 June
Source: adapted from data in Tetteh, E. and McGuiness, F. (2011) *By-elections since 2010*, House of Commons Library Standard Note SN/SG/5833.

The Leicester South by-election result provided an interesting contrast with the by-election held in the same seat back in 2004. At that time, the death of the Labour incumbent and public hostility towards UK military action in Iraq, in a constituency with a significant Muslim population, had resulted in a massive swing in favour of the Lib Dems and their candidate Parmjit Singh Gill. Though the Labour Party recaptured the seat at the 2005 general election and retained it thereafter, the scale of the swing from the Lib Dems to Labour at the 2011 by-election goes some way towards supporting the view that the Labour Party has begun to reconnect with its electoral base.

Why did some parties fare better than others?

Although parties in government at Westminster often perform badly both in by-elections and at local elections, the sheer range of elections held in 2011 and the considerable variation in outcomes are such that it is difficult to make generalisations on the question of causation.

That said, a number of conclusions would appear to be self-evident:
- While Labour have been the chief beneficiaries of the public backlash against the coalition's austerity programme, it would appear that the Lib Dems — as opposed to the Conservatives — have suffered most at the polls.
- Though the election of Ed Miliband as Labour leader in place of Gordon Brown appears to have stopped Labour's electoral rot, the party has not enjoyed the kind of electoral successes that one might have anticipated in the face of massive public sector job losses, rising inflation and stubbornly high rates of unemployment.
- The experience of a minority SNP administration in Scotland between 2007 and 2011, far from exposing the party's supposed deficiencies and thereby 'calling the nationalist bluff', appears instead to have lent them greater electoral credibility and authority.
- While the majority of Scots may still oppose full independence, they are clearly at ease with the idea of the SNP running the nation's devolved institutions. Significantly, support for what the nationalists call 'devolution max' (one step short of full independence) has increased.

Can we learn anything by studying the results in 'second order elections'?

YES
- Such contests offer a snap-shot of public opinion.
- They provide a wealth of information relating to the relative strength of political parties in different localities around the UK.
- They are often significant contests in themselves, in the sense that those public officials returned to office often wield considerable power over those who live within their jurisdictions.

- They can serve to dissuade the government of the day at Westminster from pursuing certain policies.
- They provide a useful illustration of the way in which different voting systems may contribute to different electoral outcomes.

NO

- Such elections only ever offer a partial and often unreliable indication of how parties might fair at a UK-wide general election.
- These contests are often accompanied by high levels of protest voting and low levels of electoral turnout.
- Individual seats lost as a result of massive swings against the party (or parties) in office at Westminster often revert to their 'natural party' at the next electoral opportunity.
- Parties often win back-to-back general election victories in spite of massive losses at second order elections in the intervening years.
- Many of those elected in such contests remain subject to direct control from Westminster.

Summary

- Whereas the Lib Dems suffered at the polls, the Conservative Party's support largely held up, suggesting that their coalition partners and not they themselves bore the brunt of public concern over the coalition's economic strategy.
- Labour performed relatively well in the four British by-elections held in 2011 and regained lost ground at the local elections, having experienced heavy losses in contests at this tier of government over the course of 13 years in office at Westminster.
- Though the 2011 elections to the assemblies in Wales and Northern Ireland were unremarkable, the SNP victory in Scotland could have far-reaching implications for the future of the Union.

Exam focus

To consolidate your knowledge of this chapter, answer the following questions:

1 How were the elections to the Scottish Parliament in 2011 'truly ground-breaking'?
2 Why might the government party or parties face heavy losses at local elections?
3 Who won, who lost and why in the 2011 local government elections?
4 Present the arguments for and against directly elected mayors.
5 Do by-elections matter? Give reasons to support your answer.
6 To what extent do the various elections of 2011 tell us anything about the likely outcome of the next general election?

Chapter 2

The AV Referendum: is FPTP here to stay?

Exam success

The up-to-date facts, examples and arguments in this chapter will help you to produce good-quality answers in your AS unit tests in the following areas of the specifications:

Edexcel	AQA	OCR
Unit 1	**Unit 1**	**Unit F851**
Elections	Electoral systems	Electoral systems and referenda

Context

Following the general election of 2010, all three parties were supportive of a national referendum on whether to adopt the Alternative Vote system (AV). After some controversy, Parliament legislated for the referendum to be held on 5 May 2011. After a campaign that lasted several weeks, the vote duly took place and the result was a decisive 'no' to the introduction of AV.

The national result was as follows:

	Number of votes cast	Proportion of votes
Yes to AV	6.15 million	32.1%
No to AV	13.01 million	67.9%
Turnout		42.2%

The result was a clear rejection of AV. Although the turnout, at 42.2%, demonstrated a high degree of public apathy, the scale of the defeat for the proponents of reform was resounding. The government immediately announced the abandonment of proposals for electoral reform for 'the foreseeable future'.

The nature of the campaign

Six months before the referendum, the **'Yes' campaign** was comfortably ahead in the opinion polls. However, as the campaign unfolded, opinion swung steadily against AV. If we take just one polling organisation (ICM), we can trace this change over time. This is shown in Table 2.1.

Table 2.1 The shift in opinion against AV

Date	% intending to vote yes	% intending to vote no	Don't know
28/11/10	48	35	17
20/2/11	37	37	27
17/4/11	42	58	not allowed
5/5/11 (actual result)	32	68	n/a

Certainly, as the campaign got under way it seemed that the forces backing a change were more formidable than the opposition. The 'Yes' campaign included the following important elements:

- the Liberal Democrat Party
- most of the Labour Party
- a few 'dissident' Conservatives
- the nationalist parties
- the Green Party
- UKIP
- the pressure group Liberty
- the pressure group The Electoral Reform Society
- the pressure group Unlock Democracy
- the *Guardian*, *Independent*, *Daily Mirror* and *Financial Times* newspapers

The forces ranged in the **'No' campaign** looked meagre by contrast. These included:

- the Conservative Party
- the British National Party (BNP)
- the Democratic Unionist Party in Northern Ireland
- some large trade unions
- the *Sun*, *Times*, *Daily Mail*, *Daily Express* and *Daily Telegraph* newspapers
- a few dissident members of the Labour Party

In addition, at the beginning of the campaign David Cameron claimed that the 'No' campaign was not a Conservative Party campaign, even though he and his party opposed the change. This certainly weakened the 'no' position.

The turning point in the campaign came in February 2011. Two factors were at work. First, Cameron changed his position and now accepted that the 'No' campaign was indeed the Conservative Party's official position. The second was the claim that the change would cost £250 million. Although the figure was plainly wrong and based on false assumptions, it captured the public imagination and was never effectively combated.

To some extent, also, Cameron outflanked his opposition by campaigning hard for other political reforms, notably reducing the size of the House of Commons, making constituency sizes more equal and giving constituents the power to 'recall' unsatisfactory MPs. The piecemeal, fragmented reforms did seem to satisfy many of the public demands for reform to deal with the crisis of confidence in Parliament that followed the MPs' expenses scandals.

By March 2011, the 'No' campaign was enjoying a bandwagon effect and by the end of that month the result was inevitable. Running rapidly out of hope, the 'Yes' campaign lost impetus and headed for inevitable defeat.

Explaining the result

The question has to be asked: why did the 'Yes' campaign fail so badly? A number of reasons suggest themselves.

- Perhaps the most popular explanation concerns the position of the Liberal Democrat Party in general and Nick Clegg in particular. Both were inextricably linked to the 'Yes' campaign and yet both had declined sharply in public esteem. The Liberal Democrats' 'U-turn' on tuition fees had been especially devastating. Many of the public apparently thought the party could not be trusted and so its judgment on electoral reform was similarly flawed.

- The 'no' vote could be seen as much a vote against coalition government as it was a rejection of AV. The public had seen a year of coalition government and they did not like much of what they had seen. The early euphoria created by the May 2010 result and its promise of a 'new style' of politics had evaporated.

- The 'Yes' campaign failed to engage sufficiently with young voters, seen as the most fertile ground for their campaign. This was partly due to the collapse in support for the Liberal Democrats among the young, but also the result of a failure to convince these voters that AV would deliver significant change.

- Though the 'No' campaign was accused of lying over such issues as the cost of implementing change and the complications of the system, the 'Yes' campaign simply failed to persuade the electorate that they were perhaps being duped. There was a failure to deal effectively with these two major claims of the 'No' campaign. The issue of cost was particularly telling at a time of growing economic austerity.

- The balance of media and celebrity opinion shifted towards a 'no' vote as time went by.

- While the 'No' campaign was dominated by a virtually united party (the Conservatives), the 'Yes' campaign was relatively fragmented as it was a broad 'rainbow' coalition of Liberal Democrats, liberal pressure groups, small parties and elements of the Labour Party. The Labour Party could scarcely disguise the splits within its own ranks. Indeed the whole 'Yes' campaign was hindered by a less enthusiastic wing who believed that AV was a compromise and the real goal was proportional representation. The Conservatives suffered from no such doubts.

- The 'No' campaign spent slightly more than the 'Yes' campaign, at £3.4 million against £2.6 million.

- It could be argued that the result once again proves that the British public are fundamentally 'conservative' (small 'c') when it comes to constitutional change.

Table 2.2 The arguments for and against AV

Arguments in favour of AV	Arguments against AV
■ It would mean that all MPs would be elected on an absolute majority of the vote in their constituencies. ■ The voters would have more choice, being able to place all candidates in their order of preference. ■ There would be fewer 'wasted' votes. ■ It held out the promise of breaking the domination of the two main parties and therefore of a new era of consensus politics. ■ Small parties would be able to have some impact on electoral politics.	■ Many voters found the proposed system too complicated. ■ There were fears that its introduction would be too costly. ■ It would place more choice and influence into the hands of voters who support small parties. ■ It could make majority government rare, with consequent political uncertainty and indecisiveness. ■ Many of the electorate prefer the retention of two-party politics.

The aftermath

The result was a major disaster for an already beleaguered Liberal Democrat Party. Its flagship policy of electoral reform had been destroyed for a generation. Already in difficulty over the tuition fees debacle and Nick Clegg's declining authority, the blow looked like a fatal one. Collapsing poll support for the Liberal Democrats, demonstrated by their heavy defeats in the local government elections of May 2011, became critical after the referendum. In particular the party lost the support of virtually all young voters.

It was also a blow for Labour, though not as serious as it had been for the Liberal Democrats. It showed up dissension in the party over electoral reform and so it was presented as a disunited party.

It was something of a triumph for David Cameron. Though he distanced himself from direct involvement with the 'No' campaign, the victory was seen as his to a great extent.

Nevertheless, an unexpected outcome of the referendum has not advantaged the Conservatives. With the loss of electoral reform, the Liberal Democrats were forced to impose themselves on the coalition in other areas. In other words, thwarted on AV, they turned their attention to other key areas, notably the reform of the NHS and the banking system. Desperate to re-engage with voters and their own core support, they needed to demonstrate their effectiveness. Far from being cowed by defeat, the Liberal Democrats have come out fighting, making governing with a coalition much more difficult.

What will happen to electoral reform?

Despite the end of the AV debate, electoral reform remains on the political agenda. In particular, there will be a debate concerning the electoral system to be used for a reformed, elected House of Lords. This is likely to be some form of proportional representation. Similarly, there may be proposals for reform of elections in local government. Scotland and Northern Ireland already use the Single Transferable Vote (STV) for their local elections and this may also be exported to Wales, especially when the Welsh Assembly claims greater political autonomy after 2012. There is also some debate over English local government.

However, the debate over reform of the system for general elections seems to be over for at least a generation. Even if one or two parties were to revive the debate, it seems unlikely that the British public would approve of it.

What will happen to the two-party system?

In many ways, the AV referendum 'no' vote can be seen as a rejection of three-party politics and coalition government. Similarly, it can be viewed as an endorsement of two-party politics. Of course, the paradox of the 2010 general election was that the first-past-the-post (FPTP) system produced an indecisive result. A year later, an equally strange occurrence took place when the partially proportional Additional Member System (AMS) in Scotland produced an overall majority for the Scottish National Party (SNP) in the Scottish parliamentary election. In other words, both FPTP and AMS produced results for which they were *not* designed.

In some ways, these 'perverse' results in the UK and Scotland tend to support the status quo. What they signified was that the result of an election is *not* determined by the nature of the electoral system. Instead it is the result of public sentiment. The UK did not elect a single-party government in 2010 because there was insufficient support for *either* major party. Similarly, the Scottish result was the natural outcome of a surge in nationalist sentiment and support for the SNP's popular leader, Alex Salmond.

Assuming, then, that May 2010 was indeed a 'freak' result, the future of two-party politics in the UK looks to be secure. The dramatic fall in support for the Liberal Democrats since that election will add further weight to the popularity of two-party politics. The mould of British politics does not appear to have been broken and normal service is likely to be resumed in 2015.

Was the AV referendum a success?

It could be said that the AV referendum of May 2011 was a resounding success. It produced a clear result that resolved a major political controversy. It also prevented the government from introducing a reform that did not command widespread public support. In other words, direct democracy seemed to be the winner. If we scratch the surface, however, we can detect some flaws in the democratic process. Among them are the following:

- The result may well have been determined not by the actual issue, but was used by the electorate as a way of punishing the Liberal Democrats for their ineffective performance in the coalition.
- There was a good deal of evidence that the campaigns, especially the 'No' campaign, produced distortions of the true implications of reform.
- The result may have been determined more by the better organisation and funding of the 'No' campaign than by the nature of the debate itself.
- Most of the print media were opposed to AV so there was not a 'level playing field'.
- The choice presented to the public was perhaps too limited because there had to be a simple 'yes' or 'no' answer. In other words, had the public been presented with a range of options (including, for example, some forms of proportional representation), rather than just two, the debate may well have been more sophisticated and open.

Summary

The question posed at the beginning of this chapter was 'Is FPTP here to stay?' The answer has to be, for the foreseeable future, yes. Electoral reform cannot be placed on the political agenda again until memories of the referendum campaign have faded. The result of the referendum left all politicians in no doubt about the public mood. All three major parties have accepted that the issue is, for the moment, dead. The key points in this chapter have been:

- The referendum produced a very clear result that settled the debate over electoral reform.
- The referendum result may have been distorted by the unpopularity of Nick Clegg and the Liberal Democrat Party.
- The referendum result may also have been affected by the relative success of the 'No' campaign.
- The referendum result represents a vote of confidence in the first-past-the-post system as well as in the two-party system that is usually its outcome.

Exam focus

To consolidate your knowledge of this chapter, answer the following questions:

1 Why was the issue of the introduction of the Alternative Vote for UK general elections put to the public in a referendum?
2 What were the main arguments for and against the introduction of the AV system?
3 What were likely to have been the main consequences of the introduction of the Alternative Vote?
4 Assess the relative merits of two-party and three-party systems.
5 What are the main advantages of using a referendum to determine important political issues?

Chapter 3

Coalition government: is it working?

Exam success

The up-to-date facts, examples and arguments in this chapter will help you to produce good-quality answers in your AS unit tests in the following areas of the specifications:

Edexcel	AQA	OCR
Unit 2	**Unit 2**	**Unit F852**
The prime minister and cabinet	The core executive	The executive

Context

The Conservative–Liberal Democrat coalition that came into being in May 2010 has survived longer than many commentators believed possible. After a shaky start, it seems to have gathered strength, so much so that by the end of 2011 there appeared to be little prospect of a collapse. That said, there are pitfalls ahead and unforeseen events may well be enough to derail it. The questions examined here are:

- Is coalition working?
- Is it popular?
- Can it survive for the full 5-year-term of office?

What is coalition government?

Now that most of the 'rules' of coalition government have been allowed to develop, we can summarise what a coalition government actually is and how it operates. The main principles are as follows.

1 Clearly it is a government of more than one party, in this case two. The coalition has not faced the need to recruit any other party in order to preserve its parliamentary majority on any issue.

2 Ministerial posts are shared between the two parties. The allocation of posts between the two parties is roughly in line with their relative representation in the House of Commons. This means there are 18 Conservative cabinet members and five from the Liberal Democrats. The proportion of ministerial posts as a whole (i.e. cabinet and non-cabinet posts) shared by the parties is on a similar ratio.

3 In nearly every government department, there is at least one Liberal Democrat minister — either the department head or at least one junior minister. This ensures that the junior partner in the coalition is represented in all areas of government responsibility.

4 Where there is a need to replace a minister, the proportion of posts held by each party will be maintained and all appointments will be subject to discussion between both party leaders, David Cameron and Nick Clegg. However, the prime minister retains the ultimate decision as this remains one of his prerogative powers.

5 Liberal Democrat leader Nick Clegg is deputy prime minister. This means he deputises for David Cameron when he leaves the country or is indisposed (for example when Cameron went on paternity leave). This does not, however, mean that the deputy prime minister becomes chief policy maker in the prime minister's absence. It means that he makes himself accountable to Parliament and the media on behalf of the government.

6 The official policy of the coalition is contained in the 'coalition agreement', drafted in 2010. This agreement provides policy guidelines but is not official government policy. It effectively replaces the party manifesto in a single-party government.

7 The leaderships of the two parties discuss and announce their party policies separately. However, official government policy must be ratified by the cabinet. All coalition ministers are still bound by collective responsibility, meaning they must defend cabinet policy. However, while policy is being formulated, ministers may disagree publicly.

8 Ministers are required not to vote against any government policy when it is presented in Parliament. In extreme cases, they may abstain.

9 Backbench MPs remain free to support or oppose government policy as they see fit.

What are the significant differences between coalition and single-party government?

Having established how coalition government appears to be operating, we can pick out the main changes that have occurred at the centre of government. These include:

■ In theory, the prime minister's authority is weaker than in a single-party government. This is because his party did not 'win' the election: he does not have a clear mandate and his patronage powers are weakened (see next point below). However, in practice, as is suggested in this chapter, David Cameron is proving to be perhaps as dominant as any other prime minister.

- The prime minister has new constraints on who he can appoint to ministerial posts. He must consult with his deputy and coalition partner and must maintain an appropriate balance in the representation of the two parties. In other words, his patronage powers have been slightly weakened.
- The role of the cabinet has been enhanced. Because some sensitive policies give rise to disputes between members of the two coalition parties, the cabinet is needed to declare official government policy. Thus a system of compromise and consensus building needs to take place.
- There is no longer an electoral mandate against which to judge government. Both parties (especially the Liberal Democrats) have had to renounce some election manifesto commitments. The nearest thing to a mandate is the coalition agreement, but even that is more flexible than a manifesto.
- Although the principle of collective responsibility still exists, it is considerably weakened and a certain degree of flexibility in the doctrine is inevitable.

Table 3.1 The key problems for the coalition

Issue	Strains on the coalition
Tuition fees	The Conservative Party was determined to raise tuition fees to pay for higher education. The Liberal Democrats had promised to resist such rises but were faced with the prospect of bringing down the government if they did. They chose to support the Conservatives to avoid a crisis.
Electoral reform	This was a flagship Liberal Democrat policy. The Conservatives supported a referendum campaign against reform and the failure of reform weakened the Liberal Democrat position.
NHS reform	Here again the Liberal Democrats faced a choice between bringing down the government or supporting reforms about which they were dubious. They allowed the reforms to proceed, having obtained some moderate amendments to the legislation.
Bank reform	This is driven by business secretary Vince Cable. The Liberal Democrats openly support radical measures to control banking practices, bonuses etc. but the Conservatives are reluctant to take such radical measures, fearing that banks will move abroad. This remains a point of friction between the coalition partners.

How successful has coalition government been?

It is perhaps very early to give a verdict on coalition government, but there are already interesting pieces of evidence against which to judge it. This evaluation can be carried out by answering a series of key questions.

Has it provided stable government?

The answer here has to be yes — so far. The coalition has had its shaky moments, especially in the first few months, but at present it does not look set to collapse. Policy making has been relatively untroubled. Above all, the economic and financial problems which steadily grew during 2011 did not prevent government from making key decisions. There have been some revolts in the House of Commons, but there has been no real prospect of a

government defeat. This can be contrasted with the government of John Major between 1992 and 1997, which constantly teetered on the brink of collapse and which lost a number of key votes.

Above all, it can be argued that, with so many financial and economic problems facing the developed world, unstable minority government could have been disastrous. With decisive action needed to deal with public sector debt, a degree of certainty that government would last for 5 years at least was sorely needed. This seems to have been established.

Has it created more moderate government?

One of the main arguments that is often put up in defence of coalition government is that it will be more moderate and will prevent an extreme party having too much power. There is much evidence to suggest that the coalition has indeed prevented the right wing of the Conservative Party from gaining ascendancy. In areas such as law and order, taxation, immigration, the Liberal Democrats' more moderate position has helped David Cameron keep his own right wing at bay. He has been less successful on relations with the European Union.

Has it made government more accountable?

There was an assumption that a coalition government would be more 'open' and susceptible to parliamentary scrutiny and even control. Certainly ministers have been more open about their views on policy and have been willing to criticise publicly any policies with which they did not agree. Business secretary Vince Cable, for example, has been critical of the government's failure to take more radical steps to regulate the big banks and Nick Clegg himself has openly declared his opposition to the idea of a new British Bill of Rights which has been proposed by home secretary Theresa May. On the other hand, it has also become necessary for the party leaders to do deals behind closed doors to achieve coalition approval for more controversial policies. Liberal Democrat backbench MPs have also largely failed to carry out threats to thwart government plans over tuition fees and NHS reforms. Despite the fact that a coalition government is in a more precarious position than a government with an overall majority, backbench MPs have largely failed to use their potential power to any significant extent.

Has it benefited the Liberal Democrats?

It had been hoped by Liberal Democrats and other supporters of a more open democracy that the experience of coalition government would establish the Liberal Democrats as a credible alternative party of government, thus breaking the stranglehold of the two-party system. In practice, however, the opposite has happened. Nick Clegg has failed to establish himself as a potential prime minister as he has been seen as too weak in 'giving in' to Conservative demands over such issues as student tuition fees and NHS reform. The Liberal Democrats were already discredited when they broke a firm election promise not to allow tuition fees to rise. However, when the May 2011 referendum on the introduction of the Alternative Vote produced a 'no' vote, voters clearly signalled that they had lost much faith in the party. By the autumn of 2011, the Liberal Democrats' opinion poll rating had fallen to 11%, half the level of support they had achieved in the general election. Nick Clegg also lags well behind the other two party leaders in terms of popular support and trust.

This verdict was perhaps a little harsh. The Liberal Democrats have insisted that the coalition government retain the 50% tax rate for incomes above £150,000 per annum (against strong opposition from the right wing of the Conservative Party) and that the tax-free allowance should be gradually raised to £10,000. They also introduced a number of modifications to the NHS reform proposals. Furthermore, the Liberal Democrats supported the introduction of fixed-term parliaments which David Cameron championed as a way of protecting the coalition from early defeat. However, though a number of cherished Liberal Democrat policies have been achieved, it seems the electorate is likely to punish the Lib Dems for their betrayal on tuition fees and their failure to deliver electoral reform. The verdict in the end may well be that the Liberal Democrats were too determined to remain in government to mount serious challenges to their Conservative senior partners.

Has it benefited the Conservative Party?
In one sense, the answer is a resounding yes. Without the advent of a coalition, the Conservatives faced the prospect of either struggling along as a minority government or not being in power at all. At a deeper level, however, the answer depends on one's perspective.

The adherents of the party's right wing have been dismayed by the experience of coalition. They believe the government has been unable to deal effectively with such issues as rising levels of crime, immigration and asylum, reform of welfare and the public services and problems related to the European Union. This has been because, they claim, the government has been hindered by the need to placate the forces of liberalism.

On the other hand, the adherents of the party's mainstream, represented by Cameron himself, see coalition as a great opportunity to re-establish Conservative fortunes after the humiliation of three consecutive election defeats. If the coalition government has some success, notably over deficit reduction and economic growth, they argue, it will be the Conservatives who will benefit.

Has coalition government brought the two-party system to an end?
If the opinion polls are to be believed, and if the Liberal Democrats fail to restore some of their credibility, the answer is likely to be no. Indeed, the poor record of Liberal Democrat influence on the government may well have *strengthened* support for the two-party system. Furthermore, the realisation

that a coalition government has no clear mandate from the electorate has brought the advantages of two-party politics into focus. When electoral reform also failed, it became more likely that the hung parliament and resultant coalition were no more than a 'blip' in the normal dominance of two parties.

What issues threaten coalition unity?

The introduction of a fixed term, at least for this parliament, means that the coalition may expect to be reasonably stable and may well survive for 5 years. However, a number of issues may well threaten coalition unity. These include:

- Conservative proposals for a 'British Bill of Rights' to replace the Human Rights Act would certainly create a major rift between the parties. The Liberal Democrats are totally committed to the Human Rights Act and Nick Clegg has declared his determination to defend it.
- David Cameron's use of the UK veto at the Brussels summit in December made Britain's relations with the European Union a major threat to coalition unity. Nick Clegg and senior Liberal Democrats were furious, accusing the prime minister of isolating the UK in Europe and damaging the national interest. The big divisive issue for the coalition in 2012?
- Law and order remains a problem. As things stand, the liberal wing of the Conservative Party, led by Kenneth Clarke, has the initiative on this issue. However, should the right wing, led by Theresa May and Liam Fox, gain the ascendancy, there is the potential for considerable conflict. The resignation of Liam Fox as defence secretary in October 2011 may, however, weaken the right wing (though, as a backbencher, Fox may well become a more serious Conservative thorn in the government's side).
- As things stand, there is inter-party agreement on how to deal with the government debt problem, but should there be a serious economic recession, this consensus might come under strain.

Table 3.2 Summary of coalition government's 'successes' and 'failures'

Perceived coalition successes	Perceived coalition failures
It has reduced the influence of 'extremists' in the Conservative Party.	The Liberal Democrats do not appear to have used their potential influence successfully.
It has prevented a potential period of political instability.	It has weakened the principle of 'manifesto and mandate', creating confusion within the electorate.
There is more openness in government when ministers disagree over policy.	It has slowed down the process of government, especially at a time of financial crisis, because of the need to obtain agreement between two parties.
Some argue it has reduced the power of the prime minister by promoting more collective government.	It can be argued that government is less open because 'deals' have to be done between the party leaders behind 'closed doors'.

Summary

Is coalition government working? There are two perspectives to this question. If we are asking whether coalition government is proving to be stable, is likely to survive and is enabling government to govern, we must reach the conclusion that it is working. On the other hand, if we are asking whether it is a genuine power-sharing arrangement and whether it has achieved widespread public approval, there must be serious doubts.

The key points in this chapter have been:

- The main feature of the coalition experience is that it has survived longer than many expected.
- Coalition is proving a painful experience for the Liberal Democrats, but has been largely successful for the Conservatives.
- The operation of coalition government is different from single-party government, but not radically so and the doctrine of collective responsibility has survived.
- Coalition government looks slightly more 'moderate' and 'liberal' than a pure Conservative government would have been.
- Policy making is more complex in a coalition, but most policy conflicts have been successfully resolved.

Exam focus

To consolidate your knowledge of this chapter, answer the following questions:

1 What new problems does coalition present for government?
2 How does coalition government affect the position of the prime minister and cabinet?
3 Does Britain still have a two-party system?
4 How are parties affected by coalition government?
5 Has coalition government strengthened or weakened the two-party system?

Chapter 4

Ed Miliband: a new direction for Labour?

Exam success

The up-to-date facts, examples and arguments in this chapter will help you to produce good-quality answers in your AS unit tests in the following areas of the specifications:

Edexcel	AQA	OCR
Unit 1	Unit 1	Unit F851
Party policies and ideas	Political parties	Political parties

Context

Following a leadership contest in 2010, in which his main rival was his brother David, Ed Miliband became the new Labour leader. Relatively little was known about his political philosophy, save for a very generalised belief that he was slightly to the left of his brother and therefore, by implication, of Tony Blair and Gordon Brown. The Labour Party was somewhat traumatised by its election defeat in May 2011 and the unpleasant experience of seeing support for its previous leader, Gordon Brown, steadily evaporating.

Labour faced a number of dilemmas in 2010–11:

1 how to respond to the new Conservative–Liberal Democrat coalition government

2 how to respond to the growing financial and economic problems caused by the 'debt crisis' in the UK and elsewhere

3 whether to continue the Blair–Brown agenda of seeking to maintain the support of 'middle Britain' through moderate consensus policies or whether to move to the left to attempt to regain some of its lost 'grass roots' support among the traditional working classes and ethnic minorities

4 how far the party should go in accepting its own contribution to the 'debt crisis' and its own failures in reducing poverty and inequality during its 13 years in office between 1997 and 2010

During the first year of his leadership, relatively little was heard about Miliband's philosophy. However, in a groundbreaking speech to the Labour Party conference in September 2011, he explained his beliefs more clearly.

Miliband's speech

The key elements of Miliband's speech are outlined below.

Benefits reform
He accepted that too little had been done under Labour to prevent people simply living off benefits and making no attempt to work. Miliband therefore hopes to renew the attack on so-called 'benefits scroungers'.

Wealth creators versus 'asset strippers'
Miliband wants to draw a clear distinction between individuals and enterprises that create wealth and employment by developing products and services, training the workforce and innovating, and companies whose sole *raison d'être* is to make money for themselves and their shareholders and whom he describes as 'asset strippers'. The distinction will be drawn by regulating the latter and forcing them to pay higher taxes. The former — the wealth creators — should not suffer excessive regulation and their contribution will be recognised through a sympathetic tax system.

Tuition fees
Miliband made a specific commitment to reducing maximum tuition fees from £9,000 per annum to £6,000 per annum. At the same time, he aspired to open more university places to young people from deprived backgrounds, though it is not clear how this is to be achieved.

High salaries
Miliband stressed that the 'excessively' high salaries paid to many at the top of industry must be curbed. He proposed that ordinary employees should be represented on company 'pay committees' to prevent senior executives simply voting themselves very high salaries.

Social housing
Apart from hoping to increase the amount of subsidised social housing available, Miliband also suggested that those who make a positive contribution to society should be given priority when social housing is being offered.

The NHS
Miliband placed the values of the NHS at the centre of his belief system. He would return the NHS to its original principles and not allow commercial interests to influence the way the service operates.

Is Miliband different from New Labour?

Here we return to the original question: do the leadership and beliefs of the new Labour represent a new departure? Table 4.1 summarises the position.

Table 4.1 New Labour and Ed Miliband compared

Policy area	New Labour	Miliband's position	Verdict
Debt reduction	At first, New Labour believed strongly in fiscal responsibility, but gradually moved towards high expenditure, especially on public services.	Miliband talks about fiscal responsibility and 'living within the country's means'.	No real distinction
Economic management	New Labour stressed the need to keep corporate taxes low and to reduce regulation to promote growth.	Miliband takes a similar position, though he is not prepared to support the elements of the economy that do not create real growth such as speculators, commodity traders and the like.	Miliband is slightly to the left of New Labour, but not fundamentally.
Trade Unions	New Labour was content to see unions relatively weak.	Miliband would not restore trade union power and opposes the use of strikes to protest about public service cuts.	No distinction
Taxation	New Labour saw taxes as a disincentive to work and enterprise and so sought to reduce direct taxes, especially those on business.	Miliband wants the tax system to discriminate clearly between those who create wealth and economic growth, and those who simply seek to make profits for themselves.	Miliband is slightly to the left of New Labour
Welfare reform	New Labour talked a great deal about 'making work pay' and creating greater incentives to work, but largely failed to achieve these aspirations.	Though Miliband has few new plans, he intends to deliver on his commitments, something he admits New Labour failed to do.	No major distinction
Inequality	New Labour assumed that creating greater equality of opportunity and improving education would reduce inequality; however, relatively little was achieved.	Miliband does have some new initiatives: he hopes to curb excessive pay at the top and also claims he will open up higher education to more families.	In terms of rhetoric at least, Miliband is to the left of New Labour: he does hope to deliver more effectively on measures to reduce inequality.
Health and education	New Labour was committed to improving both and increased expenditure on them dramatically.	There is no discernible difference in Miliband's position.	No real distinction
Other policy areas			Miliband's position remains relatively unknown on other issues; by the end of 2011, it seemed clear he proposes no major departures from traditional positions.

Does Ed Miliband have a distinctive philosophy?

There are signs that Miliband is trying to carve out a new philosophical position, a position that is appropriate for what might be termed the 'post financial crisis world'. Some of the elements of this are:

- He is trying to make clear distinctions between those who make a negative contribution to society and those whose contribution is positive. These distinctions are shown below:

Negative contributors	Positive contributors
Property speculators	Community voluntary groups
Financial speculators	Those who work hard for low pay
Companies that 'rig' markets	Wealth-creating capitalists
'Greedy' energy companies	'Ethical' employers
Investment banking	Employers who offer staff training
Asset-stripping companies	Front-line workers in public services
Overpaid company executives	
Insensitive employers	
Employers who fail to train staff	
Firms who operate with poor 'values'	
Benefits 'cheats'	

- He is calling for a new value system in society, moving away from self-seeking 'greed' towards the ethics of hard work, care for communities, environmental concern and a society that rewards 'positive' values rather than merely 'selfish' ones.
- He hopes to break the link between corporate interests and politicians who have a vested interest in maintaining their own power. He believes the relationship between the two is unhealthy and has led to inequality and an over-emphasis on wealth for the few rather than social justice.
- He has placed social justice and the reduction of inequality at the centre of his philosophy.

Miliband's legacy from New Labour

Ed Miliband remains, fundamentally, part of the New Labour legacy left by Tony Blair and Gordon Brown. He has shown a certain degree of new thinking, as shown above, but he is also a conventional centre to centre-left politician. The following features of his belief system can be seen as indications that he is *not* striking out in a markedly new direction:

- He remains a strong believer that free-market capitalism is still the most effective way of creating wealth.
- He accepts that the state does not create wealth, but can only provide welfare and distribute wealth in a more just way.
- He is committed to individualism rather than collectivism. He believes that individuals prefer to pursue their goals rather than doing so collectively.
- His main commitment to collectivism lies in education, health and the benefits system.

- He understands that taxation can be a disincentive to work and enterprise and so should be raised in a just and responsible way, avoiding the possibility of stifling enterprise.
- He is a communitarian. This means he believes that people's sense of 'society' is largely based on their communities — local, ethnic and cultural.
- He does not seek to restore the traditional powers of trade unions.

Summary

The evidence so far available suggests that Ed Miliband is not pursuing a radically new direction for Labour. He is hoping to change the *emphasis* of Labour policy. The most striking element of this is an attempt to differentiate between 'good' and 'bad' capitalism. He is also trying to persuade his party that free-market forces should not be accepted uncritically, but should be judged on a moral basis. He also promises to introduce a new 'politics' where senior politicians do not tie themselves to vested interests such as large corporations, media empires or wealthy individuals. It should be said, however, that virtually all politicians promise a new kind of 'cleaner' politics.

A further word of caution concerns the 'debt crisis'. Opposition politicians have some difficulty in establishing economic and financial policy because they are unsure about what kind of economic situation they would inherit if they won power at the next election. We have therefore heard relatively little about long-term economic plans (save for a general commitment to growth) from Miliband.

The key points in this chapter have been:

- It is very early to make firm judgements on Ed Miliband.
- He seems to be moving gradually to the left of the New Labour position.
- He is concerned with the introduction of more morality, both in the capitalist system and in the way politics is conducted.
- Miliband has not yet declared himself fully on future economic policy, mainly because the economic future is so uncertain.

Exam focus

To consolidate your knowledge of this chapter, answer the following questions:

1 Is New Labour now an outdated concept?
2 How far has Ed Miliband departed from the New Labour tradition?
3 To what extent do Labour Party policies differ from those of the coalition?
4 What is the modern Labour Party's attitude to capitalism?

Chapter 5

Pressure groups: how democratic are direct action and mass protest?

Exam success

The up-to-date facts, examples and arguments in this chapter will help you to produce good-quality answers in your AS unit tests in the following areas of the specifications:

Edexcel	AQA	OCR
Unit 1	**Unit 1**	**Unit F851**
Pressure groups	Pressure groups and protest movements	Pressure groups

Context

Recent years have seen the rise of many new movements that are campaigning on a wide range of public issues from airport expansion to tax avoidance, from anti-globalisation to protests over hospital closures. What distinguishes these new phenomena, sometimes known as 'new social movements', is that they have broken away from many of the traditional methods adopted by pressure groups, preferring forms of action often described as 'direct action'. These groups have been facilitated by the development of the internet, mobile phone technology (including smart phones) and social media such as Facebook and Twitter. The new media and communication systems have made it possible to organise action much more effectively and quickly. That these social movements have become a key part of the political landscape is not in doubt. More contentious, however, is the question of whether they enhance our democracy or threaten to undermine it.

Background

Of course the idea of mass protest, direct action and civil disobedience is nothing new. The trade union movement has always adopted the strike or other forms of industrial action to reinforce its campaigns. The Suffragettes famously were happy to go to prison to further their cause for women's suffrage early in the twentieth century. In more recent times, the environmental campaign group Greenpeace pioneered the use of 'gesture' politics to publicise its issues. Greenpeace has variously been engaged in disrupting whale hunting, destroying genetically modified crops and hindering oil exploration in areas of high environmental sensitivity. Similarly, for many years the Animal

Liberation Front has often lived up to its name by illegally releasing animals used for scientific experimentation. Various anti-foxhunting groups have also sabotaged hunting in order to undermine what they consider to be a cruel sport.

What is different today is that these kinds of actions have become more frequent, better organised, wide ranging and well supported. It has become possible to start an entirely new movement very quickly through new social media and similarly easy to organise protest via mass communications.

Who are the new groups?

Table 5.1 illustrates these developments by identifying some important examples of new movements, together with their aims and typical methods.

Table 5.1 Examples of new protest and campaign movements

Movement	Aims	Typical methods
Countryside Alliance	To prevent legislation banning various kinds of hunting, mainly fox hunting with dogs; also to raise awareness of the need to protect agriculture and the countryside	Disrupting central London by massing supporters in the streets, many on horseback
Fathers 4 Justice	To seek greater rights for fathers who have become separated from partners and thus have been denied custodial rights to their own children	Famously, leading members have dressed up as super-heroes and occupied prominent places on public buildings to gain maximum publicity
UK Uncut	To raise awareness that many wealthy individuals and companies avoid paying tax, often legally; this is especially highlighted during the current financial crisis and recession	Mainly occupying the premises of companies they believe to be avoiding tax, such as Topshop, Boots and HSBC; they have tagged onto wider protest movements to gain additional publicity
Plane Stupid	To prevent the expansion of airports, which threaten the environment and degrade the countryside	Disrupting airport development, often by occupying key pieces of land, invading airports and disrupting air transport generally
The Anti-Fuel-Tax Movement	This loose confederation of largely local groups campaigns against high taxes on vehicle fuel	Especially when there are sharp rises in fuel prices, the movement organises mass protests that disrupt vehicular movement on major roads by organising large groups of motorists and truck drivers to congregate and drive slowly in large convoys

TaxPayers' Alliance	One of the more formal organisations, it campaigns against high taxation and seeks to root out wastefulness in government	This does not use illegal activity (for example by refusing to pay taxes, though that may be used in future), but encourages members to use freedom of information legislation to publicise examples of wasteful public expenditure at local, regional and national levels
Indignant movement	This is a multi-issue movement that emerged in 2011 expressing general discontent about the operation of modern capitalism; the main targets are the international banks and multinational corporations. In the USA, the 'Occupy Wall Street' movement is part of this development	Usually it organises street protests, but semi-permanent 'camps' have also been set up in New York and London; the purpose of the camps is to raise awareness of the various issues with which the movement is concerned

What do these groups have in common?

Every campaign group is different, but there are some features that they all demonstrate. Examples of these common features include:

- Mainly, they tend to concentrate on horizontal rather than vertical organisation. This means they tend to be mass movements with many members, but few officials and administrators. Some, like the Countryside Alliance and the TaxPayers' Alliance, do have formal organisations, but these are relatively small. In general, they rely on the fact that there are many members or supporters who are willing to be highly active.
- They are 'outsider' pressure groups. This means they do not have close links with government at any level. This is partly deliberate — they do not wish to be associated with governments, but rather wish to maintain independence — and partly because governments usually do not see them as democratically 'legitimate'.
- They engage in 'gesture politics'. This relates to a variety of devices that are designed to gain maximum publicity. Typical methods involve stunts, law breaking and shock tactics, such as damage to property.
- They all seek to mobilise public opinion in their favour. This is the main way in which they hope to put pressure on government.
- It would be wrong to say that all protest movements and new social movements use illegal methods. Many do not and condemn them. However, it is a common feature of their activities, whether it be deliberate or 'collateral' law breaking, which is the consequence of robust campaigning.
- They rely heavily upon the internet, social media and mobile phone technology to mobilise action, recruit supporters and create a sense of 'community', even in the absence of formal membership or organisation.
- Few of the groups and movements are well funded. They therefore rely upon the resources of their own members and supporters. Indeed, in most cases, it is their mass support that represents their principal resource.

Why have protest movements become so important?

There is no doubt that the whole landscape of pressure group politics has been transformed over the last two decades. Every year, there are more movements springing up and more incidents in which they have become involved. 2011 certainly represents a high point in direct action and protest in British politics. Why has this happened? A number of causes can be detected, including the following:

- It may be seen as a symptom of a breakdown in traditional political processes. Parliament has long been seen as relatively 'weak' in the face of powerful, executive government. Parties have also been marginalised in policy processes. Government policy is seen to be increasingly in the hands of small, close-knit political elites. Even large, traditional pressure groups, such as trade unions and other professional associations, seem to be increasingly ignored by policy makers. Direct action and protest movements, therefore, have grown up to fill these gaps in the democratic process.

- To a large extent, the new movements have been technology-driven. In other words, they have grown up because they became *possible*. The internet, social media and mobile phone technology have meant that it is possible to recruit and mobilise large numbers of people in response to an issue. It also means that the groups can act quickly and can also avoid too much control by law enforcement agencies because they can organise themselves relatively secretly. The internet and its various manifestations have meant that people have become more informed about controversial issues than ever before.

- Globalisation has been an important factor. Increasingly, issues cross national boundaries — for example, the environment, the behaviour of capitalism, transport, European Union issues — so campaign movements must also be transnational. Traditional pressure groups were mainly *national* in nature. The new movements are not inhibited by national boundaries.

- The global financial and economic crises from 2008 onwards have heightened awareness of major problems with modern capitalism, which is sometimes seen as being 'in crisis'.

- There has been a growth in *local* protest movements too. This is again largely internet-driven. Indeed, we now often see protesters and campaigners from various parts of the country attracted to local movements, swelling their ranks and gaining them greater publicity.

Protest in 2011

2011 was a high point in protest movement activity. Table 5.2 includes a number of examples of major campaigns in 2011.

Table 5.2 Major protest campaigns in 2011

Issue	Groups involved	Methods and incidents
The growth in air transport and its resultant emissions was being seen as a major cause of climate change	Plane Stupid	The group infiltrated Manchester Airport, delaying a number of flights by obstructing aircraft
The government proposed to sell to private organisations large parts of the National Forest under the control of the Forestry Commission	An umbrella group called 38 Degrees was set up to coordinate a large number of local protest groups	A 450,000-signature petition against the sell-off was organised; many local groups organised protests and harassed government ministers, so the policy was abandoned
Information was released concerning large companies who were avoiding tax in the UK	UK Uncut	In March, a number of banks and businesses in London's Oxford Street, accused of tax avoidance, were occupied by campaigners, with considerable damage done
Government cuts and rises in university tuition fees	A campaign was originally launched by the Trade Union Congress but was joined by the National Campaign Against Fees and Cuts, a coalition of more extreme campaign groups	The 26 March demonstration was one of the largest seen in London, with up to 500,000 protesters on show; mostly a peaceful march and rally but breakaway campaigners set fire to some buildings and caused damage to property, often clashing with police lines
In September, a traveller site in Dale Farm in Essex was to be cleared by the local authority	A large number of campaign groups and anarchists joined the travellers	Protesters refused to move and had to be forcibly removed from the site, after a long series of legal challenges and judicial reviews, resulting in considerable national publicity
In the autumn of 2011, the new 'Indignant movement' set up 'camps' near St Paul's Cathedral and in the City of London	A loose collection of students, unemployed youth, socialists, anarchists and environmentalists	On the whole, in the UK, it is a peaceful movement, though there have been arrests for 'violent' and 'obstructive' behaviour in New York and Athens; the main UK method is the setting-up of protest camps

In addition to these more dramatic examples, protests were seen in 2011 against the following (protests which are likely to grow in 2012 and beyond):

- the development of a new high-speed rail system in England
- sharp rises in petrol prices
- the expansion of nuclear energy production in the UK
- reform of the disability benefits system, tightening the rules under which the disabled may claim state benefits
- new planning laws that threaten to allow industrial or retail developments to spread into areas of natural beauty and amenity
- the failure of the UK government to introduce effective bank regulation

In what ways do direct action and protest movements enhance democracy?

There are a number of positive elements to these developments in terms of the health of British democracy. We need to bear in mind, before identifying those elements, what the marks of a 'strong democracy' are. A general agreement would be that a healthy democracy is pluralistic in nature and there is widespread participation by citizens. Democracy also requires an informed citizenry. Government is expected to be sensitive to clear public demands and to be accountable for its actions. Finally, there is a strong expectation that both individual and minority rights should be respected. In the light of these considerations, the following positive elements can be identified:

- It is certainly true that the movements have brought many new participants into politics. Individuals who would perhaps never think of joining a political party, and may not even vote, have become active and politicised.
- In pluralist democracies, power is widely dispersed rather than concentrated in a few hands. The mass movements described above have certainly gone some way to spreading power and influence more widely. Groups such as UK Uncut, Plane Stupid and 38 Degrees have had some success in changing government policy, sometimes against powerful vested interests.
- Although there is a general perception that both political parties and Parliament in general are relatively weak in relation to executive power, large, successful protest movements have been able to call government to account by highlighting the adverse results of some policies. In some cases, there has been a reversal of policy (e.g. over the proposed selling to the private sector of publicly owned woodland) or important amendments to legislation (for example, additional measures added to the tuition fee policies, ensuring that more disadvantaged young people have access to top universities).
- Minority groups, when well organised, can protect themselves against discriminatory policies. The success of the Countryside Alliance has been a good example of this effect. The interests of the rural community can no longer be ignored by metropolitan politicians.
- Finally, it can be argued that the new movements have an educational function. They inform the public about issues that may have been ignored or concealed by government. This is one of the main objectives, for example, of Greenpeace and UK Uncut.

In what ways do such movements threaten democracy?

Nonetheless, the picture is far from completely positive. Table 5.3 details examples of how the activities of protest movements have possibly subverted the democratic process.

Table 5.3 How protest and other mass movements can undermine democracy

Activity	Why democracy was undermined
The Countryside Alliance's campaign against anti-fox-hunting legislation	Though the Alliance could claim it was protecting an important minority — those involved in hunting — Parliament had decisively voted for a ban and there was clear evidence that the majority of the country wanted to see foxhunting, and other forms of hunting, banned. The watering-down of the legislation did not really accord with majority public opinion.
National Campaign Against Fees and Cuts	This alliance of direct activists attached itself to a peaceful demonstration by trade unionists, students and other political groups and gained publicity through acts of civil disobedience and violence. It could be argued that seeking political change through illegal acts is fundamentally undemocratic.
Plane Stupid	Plane Stupid, campaigning against the expansion in civil aviation, is ranged against other interests that hope to see an expansion in air transport as this will benefit the British economy, creating, among other things, more employment opportunities. It can be argued that this group is not democratically accountable and so does not take into account the consequences of its protests if they prove to be successful.
The Dale Farm protest	The travellers at Dale Farm, Essex, were removed because they had not obtained official local planning permission for their settlement. It is a principle of a democracy that the rule of law should apply, so the travellers should have sought planning consent in the same way as other people must. The protesters were pleading a special case for this small group. This may be seen as an attempt to protect a minority, but it also threatened the operation of the rule of law.

Summary

Do these developments represent extensions or threats to democracy? Two conclusions, which are contradictory, can be offered. First, they can be seen in a positive light in that they are bringing more people into politics and are going some way to dispersing power more widely. Second, they can be seen in a negative light in that they may be having the effect of subverting democracy rather than strengthening it.

This chapter has therefore raised some issues in respect of protest movements and direct action. The key points have been:

- There has been considerable recent growth in the number and frequency of such movements.
- To a great extent, they have been facilitated by the use of the internet and social media.
- Groups and movements of this kind have had considerable success in influencing public opinion and government policy.
- In many ways they have improved democracy in the UK, in particular encouraging greater participation as well as dispersing power and influence more widely.
- Nevertheless, some aspects of their activities can be viewed as anti-democratic, in particular because they may subvert legitimate political processes.

Exam focus

To consolidate your knowledge of this chapter, answer the following questions:

1 What are 'new social movements' and why have they become important?
2 Why, and in what ways, have pressure groups and campaign movements adopted new methods?
3 To what extent have new campaign groups and protest movements become more successful than 'traditional' pressure groups?
4 To what extent is the 'politics of protest' democratic in nature?
5 Do pressure groups in general enhance or threaten democracy?

Chapter 6

The Big Society: what does it mean?

Exam success

The up-to-date facts, examples and arguments in this chapter will help you to produce good-quality answers in your AS unit tests in the following areas of the specifications:

Edexcel	AQA	OCR
Unit 1	**Unit 1**	**Unit F851**
Party policies and ideas	Political parties	Political parties

Context

The idea of the 'Big Society' was unveiled to the public in the Conservative Party's 2010 election manifesto. It was very much the product of David Cameron's own political philosophy, but was also an attempt to signal that the Conservative Party was moving towards a more 'liberal' position and to throw off the widely held view that it was the 'nasty party'. It can also be argued that it was part of Cameron's determination to distance himself from the party's 'Thatcherite' tradition. The main architect of the specific proposals was Nat Wei, one of Cameron's advisers.

What are the origins of Big Society?

A number of philosophical origins for the Big Society can be identified. These include:

- **Anti big government.** Conservatives have always been suspicious of over-powerful government. Big Society is, to some extent, an attempt to encourage local, voluntary action to achieve social 'good' as a replacement for the centralised 'nanny' state.
- **Liberalism.** The growing liberal tendency in the modern Conservative Party has been influenced by the view that, where action is based locally, rather than nationally, it is likely to be more democratically controlled, more accountable and more sensitive to the needs of communities.
- **Anti-Thatcherism.** The New Right (also known as neoliberalism or Thatcherism) underemphasised the importance of social ties, concentrating instead on the importance of individualism and free markets. Big Society combats this perception of conservatism, though it does not see society in 'macro' or national terms, but rather in terms of local community ties. In other words, locally-based social action need not interfere with individualism.

- **Communitarianism.** David Cameron and his allies have been much influenced by Tony Blair and New Labour (though they rarely admit this). The Labour version of Big Society was called 'communitarianism'. This suggested that, though we now live in an age of individualism and the pursuit of individual goals, collectivism remains important. Man is seen as a social animal and his social sense is most effectively expressed through a sense of obligation to society at all levels. The 'community' can be local, regional or national, but all citizens owe an obligation to strengthen community ties even while they are pursuing their own ends. The centralised welfare state does this on our behalf to some extent, but we must also take personal action to care for the needs of others and society as a whole.
- **Voluntarism.** The idea of voluntarism suggests that it is more effective and desirable if social action is voluntary rather than forced upon individuals by the state. A voluntary system of social action preserves freedom, democracy and choice.

What does Big Society mean in practice?

A number of practical initiatives can be grouped together under the general heading of 'Big Society'. Among them are the following:

- free schools
- localism legislation
- reform of the NHS
- the Big Society Bank
- the National Citizen Service
- elected police commissioners
- reform of local planning laws
- recall powers for local constituents

Each of these policies is described below.

Free schools

Community and other voluntary groups now have the power to set up their own schools, either primary or secondary, which would be outside the control of both local authorities and central government. Free schools control their own staff recruitment, curricula and general education policies. They can also raise additional finance from private or charitable sources. Essentially, they fall into the control of their own parent bodies.

The free-school policy is designed to provide a higher degree of educational choice within communities. It also takes education out of government control so that there is a high degree of local democracy in schools' control. Some free schools can also specialise, for example in religious education.

In September 2011, the first 24 free schools opened. This was a modest beginning, but more free schools are planned for the future and have been approved in principle by the Department for Education.

The Localism Bill

This bill began its journey through Parliament in the autumn of 2011 and represents the flagship of the Big Society movement. It may well be amended during its legislative passage, but its main elements are as follows:

- There will be a new basis for the relationship between local councils and state regulation. In future, it will be *assumed* that a local authority has the power to take a certain action, *unless it can be proved that the action is forbidden by law*. Currently local authorities have to wait until actions are approved by central government. It is presumed that this change will increase the freedom of action of local government and will reduce central government regulation and control.
- In May 2012, major cities in England will hold referendums to determine whether they will introduce elected mayors (there are already 11 elected mayors, including in London). Elected mayors are seen as an important enhancement to local democracy and accountability.
- The London Mayor specifically will be granted additional powers which are currently in the hands of central government. These powers include control of large budgets for economic regeneration and housing provision.
- A local 'initiative' system will be introduced. This is essentially an American system where groups of citizens may demand the holding of a referendum on a local issue, provided it can be shown that there is enough support for change.
- If a local authority wishes to increase council tax by an amount that is above the government's limit, it will be forced to hold a local referendum to approve the tax rise. In so doing, a local authority will have to explain why the exceptional rise in tax is needed.
- Communities will be asked to approve a 'Neighbourhood Plan' which will map out the future physical development of the area. Any future planning decisions will have to conform to the Neighbourhood Plan.
- Communities will be consulted on how waiting lists for subsidised council housing should be constructed. In other words there will be local control over what kind of families should be prioritised in housing provision. It is generally assumed that communities will give priorities to established members of the local community.
- The procedures for local planning decisions are to be simplified and therefore speeded up.

NHS reform

This controversial legislation passed through the House of Commons in September 2011 but still faced stormy waters in the Lords. However, the basic reform remains intact.

The spending priorities of the NHS are currently largely in the hands of 'Primary Care Trusts' (PCTs). These organisations are largely controlled by professional managers and are heavily controlled by the Department of

Health. The PCTs are to be abolished and replaced by commissioning groups largely made up of general practitioners (i.e. local family doctors) and other health professionals. After Liberal Democrat-sponsored amendments, these commissioning groups will now have a local democratic element through patient representation. The reform has a number of objectives:

- There will be more local choice in health provision.
- The allocation of NHS funds will be in the hands of local health professionals rather than professional managers.
- It will broaden the range of organisations that can offer health provision and so improve patient choice.
- There will be more local democratic control over health provision in place of 'faceless' managers who may not be sensitive to local needs.

The Big Society Bank

This came into existence in July 2011. It then became 'Big Society Capital'. The organisation has initial funds amounting to £600 million to be made available to voluntary organisations and schemes that could not normally raise funds from the private banking sector and that need financial advice. It is envisaged that the investments will be used for employment and training schemes, youth projects, housing developments and the like, all community-based.

The funding comes from two main sources: investments from the four major UK high street banks, and funds from bank accounts that have remained 'dormant' or unused for a long period of time where it is assumed the money will never be reclaimed.

This scheme has still not been approved by the EU, but is expected to be approved by the end of 2011.

The National Citizen Service

This is a limited scheme to give thousands of 16-year-olds, both in and out of education, the opportunity to engage in community work for a whole summer. It is designed both to give young people skills and social awareness and to resource a variety of community initiatives.

Elected police commissioners

Police commissioners will have the task of overseeing the work and organisation of various police forces. They will seek to ensure their efficiency, effectiveness and general policies. As it is assumed that each region has its own particular crime issues, the commissioners themselves should be subject to local accountability. It is therefore proposed that each region should elect a commissioner to make law enforcement more sensitive to local needs.

Reform of local planning laws

This is largely contained in the national Planning Policy Framework, due for legislation in 2012. This highly controversial reform places a duty on local government to approve planning schemes that will promote economic growth. It is considered part of the localism and Big Society programme in that it provides greater opportunity for local enterprises to gain approval for their plans without excessive interference from government. Provided plans conform to local neighbourhood planning schemes, which are themselves subject to community approval, they are likely to be considered favourably and will not be blocked by over-bureaucratic government.

Recall powers for local constituents

The scandals over MPs' excessively claiming expenses which occurred in 2009–10 led to a general fall in public confidence in the conduct of their elected representatives. It is therefore proposed that parliamentary constituencies should have the power to demand a by-election if there are a sufficient number of citizens who show themselves to be dissatisfied with the conduct of their MP.

This is known as 'power of recall'. It is hoped that this will not only improve the conduct of MPs but will also force them to be much more accountable to local opinion. Local democracy will thus be improved.

Table 6.1 Summary of Big Society initiatives

Initiative	Objectives in terms of Big Society
Free schools	To give local people a chance to become involved in education provision, to provide more choice and more independence for individual schools
Localism legislation	To strengthen local democracy through the increased use of initiatives and referendums; to increase the amount of consultation with citizens over local plans
NHS reform	To increase local involvement in health-service decision making; to increase local choice in healthcare provision
Big Society Bank (Capital)	To provide financial capital and advice on locally based projects concerned with employment, training and similar
National Citizen Service	To engage young people with local social action and provide staffing for local environmental projects
Elected police commissioners	To improve local accountability of police services, taking account of local crime and law enforcement issues
Reform of planning laws	To reduce central government bureaucracy in planning; to provide more opportunity for local economic development
Constituency recall powers	To improve the accountability of elected MPs

Criticisms of Big Society

Not surprisingly, the Big Society idea received a great deal of criticism from the Labour Party. It was also roundly condemned by most of the large trade unions. The Liberal Democrat Party has remained cautiously supportive, though there has been concern in the party over some individual measures. The main criticisms have included the following:

- The main concern was that Big Society was merely an attempt to compensate for the effects of the huge cuts that were to be made in public expenditure from 2011 onwards, the result of the need to reduce government borrowing. Many central and local government services will suffer cuts in funding. It is claimed that attempts to encourage *voluntary* action are a means of 'papering over the cracks'.
- Big Society will not work simply because the tradition of community responsibility and volunteering in the UK is too weak. Citizens in the UK have become used to relying on the state, at central and local level, to deal with social issues such as housing, environmental protection, law and order, employment, education and social care. If these are partly withdrawn, it may be difficult to fill the gaps. On a broader scale, Big Society appears to need a deep cultural change in British society. This may take more than one generation to effect.
- Where services are controlled by the state (so-called 'top-down' government), it normally means that there is equality of service in all parts of the country. Decentralising services and putting them in local control, it can be argued, will mean large inequalities in different parts of the country. For example, schooling may improve in localities where free schools are successfully opened, but may lag behind where there are no new free schools. Similarly, NHS reform may mean a greater 'postcode lottery'. This means that some medical services may be available in some postcode areas, but not others. This could be the result of decentralising control over the allocation of health budgets.
- There is serious concern that a 'free-for-all' over local planning may result in uncontrolled developments which will degrade the local environment.
- There is a little evidence that the public have any great appetite for more referendums and consultations. Turnout in recent referendums has been disappointing (e.g. a 42% turnout in the well-publicised AV referendum of May 2011). This suggests that referendums on elected mayors, local neighbourhood plans or local taxation may be undermined by poor voting figures. Similarly, there is no guarantee that electorates will show much interest in electing mayors or police commissioners.
- A philosophical reservation to Big Society is that there will always be a tendency for government and the state to exercise control over society. In the past, many governments have offered to reduce regulation and control but none have done so. This suggests that Big Society reforms to reduce control, regulation, bureaucracy and centralisation, in favour of localism and freedom of action, will fail in the long run.

Table 6.2 Summary of the advantages and disadvantages of the
Big Society initiative

Advantages of Big Society	Disadvantages of Big Society
■ It will reduce our reliance on government at both central and local level. ■ It will foster a stronger sense of responsibility and citizenship among the British people. This will strengthen communities and help to fix the so-called 'broken society'. ■ It will create more local democracy, choice and freedom, reducing regulation from government. It will also make government more accountable. ■ It will encourage local enterprise and economic growth.	■ The quality of local services may decline, especially as government withdraws and the gap is not filled by voluntary action or the private sector. ■ Poor and disadvantaged communities will suffer because they do not have the resources to make Big Society work. This will increase inequality in living standards from one locality to another. ■ It may have only a short-run effect. It is argued that eventually the state will have to intervene as local action becomes insufficient to deal with local issues. ■ Many fear growing environmental problems as local economic development becomes less controlled.

Summary

What does Big Society mean? We might also ask, is it a coherent set of ideas? Certainly it does have a clear thrust. Andrew Heywood (*Politics Review*, September 2011) has described the movement as 'civic conservatism' and as a clear attempt to move away from free-market Thatcherism. Fundamentally, it is the endeavour to:

■ transfer a whole series of responsibilities away from government and place it in the hands of individuals, community and voluntary groups
■ decentralise government and give more power to local government
■ make local government more accountable
■ change the political culture of Britain

The change in the culture is an attempt to persuade people that they should not always look to government to solve their problems and meet their goals. Instead they should look to themselves to see what they can achieve individually and collectively. It is perhaps this change of culture that will be most difficult to achieve.

The key points in this chapter have been:

■ Big Society was a key initiative in David Cameron's attempt to introduce a 'new kind of conservatism'.
■ In theory it represents a major decentralisation of government in UK society.
■ Big Society is, to a large extent, a continuation of New Labour and liberal social policies.
■ It also conforms, to some extent, to Thatcherite conservatism, as it is designed to reduce the level of state control in society — a key neoliberal idea.
■ Critics of Big Society suggest it is largely a way of compensating for the major cuts in public expenditure being introduced by the coalition government.

Exam focus

To consolidate your knowledge of this chapter, answer the following questions:

1 In what ways and to what extent does the Big Society initiative conform to traditional conservative ideas?
2 Why did David Cameron introduce his Big Society policies in 2010?
3 On what grounds has Big Society been criticised?
4 How can Big Society help to reduce the power of government and the state?

Chapter 7

The House of Commons: a return to backbench influence?

Exam success

The up-to-date facts, examples and arguments in this chapter will help you to produce good-quality answers in your AS unit tests in the following areas of the specifications:

Edexcel	AQA	OCR
Unit 2	**Unit 2**	**Unit F852**
Parliament	Parliament	The legislature

Context

It is often said that the nineteenth century in British politics was the 'golden age' of the backbench MP. This was during a period when governments were notoriously unstable, often formed as weak coalitions, and party groupings were very loose, so that there were frequent breakdowns in party discipline. On many critical votes, groups of dissident MPs could make or break a government policy. If an issue was important enough, an adverse vote would also bring down the government. This meant that individual MPs really did have influence and were often 'courted' by party leaders to gain and maintain their support.

During the twentieth century, however, particularly after the decline of the Liberal Party in the 1930s, political reality changed. The parties became more disciplined and whips were able to maintain strong unity. The arrival of the two-party system also meant that governments often secured a comfortable majority so that even sizeable groups of dissident backbenchers could not disturb the stability of government. From 1945 to the end of the century, backbench MPs were often seen as little more than 'lobby fodder' who could be expected to be herded into the division lobbies by the whips with little complaint. Defeats on government measures were rare and largely confined to brief periods when government was operating with a very small majority (1964–66, 1974–79 and 1992–97).

The main reasons for the weakness of MPs up to 2010 are:

- The government usually enjoyed a comfortable majority in the House of Commons, so revolts by small groups of backbenchers were usually ineffective.
- Prime ministerial patronage was powerful. The fact that most backbench MPs are ambitious to become ministers and rely on the prime minister for

possible promotion meant that there was a tendency to be loyal to the party line. Loyalty has been seen as a vital quality for potential ministers.

- Dissident MPs would be reminded by the whips that continued displays of independence and defiance might ultimately bring down the government, and certainly weaken it.
- There were few opportunities in the Commons for backbenchers to raise important issues or draw the government's attention to key issues.

What has changed?

A number of developments have altered the relationship between backbench MPs and party leaders. Table 7.1 explains these changes.

Table 7.1 Developments leading to greater backbench influence

Development	Reasons for change
Coalition government	This is potentially of great importance. The coalition is intrinsically weaker than single-party government. Groups of dissident MPs, either Conservative or Liberal Democrat, can defy the government, threatening the success of some policies and legislation.
Departmental select committees	Although they have been in existence since 1979, they are becoming more influential. The membership and chairs of the committees are no longer controlled by party whips, but are determined by backbenchers themselves. The chairs receive additional salary to the normal MPs' pay (an extra £15,000 p.a.) and so may see their work as an alternative career option, free of prime ministerial control.
The Backbench Business Committee	This committee, set up in 2010, controls 35 days in the parliamentary year when it can debate issues of importance to backbenchers, rather than to the government. The committee also manages e-petitions (see digital democracy below). It is also proposed that, in future, backbench MPs will gain greater control over House of Commons business as a whole.
Professionalism	In recent years, MPs have recognised their relative political impotence and have begun to develop a new professionalism. There is a new 'breed' of backbenchers who are independent-minded and determined to pursue their own political interests.
Digital democracy	MPs can now contact large numbers of people through the internet and social media. This can give them greater authority. E-petitions have also been introduced (July 2011), whereby the House of Commons may debate an issue if 100,000 signatures are secured (see the Hillsborough disaster issue below). MPs are often leading figures behind such petitions.

Some of these developments are permanent while others are not, notably coalition government. However, it is clear that backbench MPs now do have more influence and that government ministers must pay more attention to their demands. This is examined in more detail below.

Revolts and dissidents — the Nottingham University evidence

Led by Philip Cowley, Nottingham University's parliamentary revolts unit provides interesting evidence concerning the behaviour of MPs. It has recorded the number of occasions on which *any* number of MPs of the governing party have defied the party whip by either abstaining or voting against a government proposal.

None of the data in Table 7.2 indicate that the government has actually been *defeated* by backbench action, but the trends shown suggest that backbenchers are becoming more independent-minded and more willing to defy their own party whips. MPs in general are becoming less inclined to follow the party line slavishly.

Table 7.2 The growing incidence of backbench revolts against the government

Parliamentary period	Proportion of votes where *some* MPs of the governing party voted against their own party line
1997–2001	8%
2001–05	21%
2005–10	28%
May 2010–September 2011	44% (MPs of both coalition partners)

Source: www.revolts.co.uk

Independent backbench MPs — some case studies

Here we look at some examples from the current parliament of backbench MPs who are making a significant impact of one kind or another.

Graham Allen – Labour – Nottingham North

Allen is currently chairman of the backbench Political and Constitutional Reform Committee. He is thus a champion of reform, notably of the electoral system (now a largely dead issue — see Chapter 2) and an elected House of Lords. He is also an advocate of a codified constitution. He was a key member of the Wright Committee on reform of the House of Commons, which did create several reforms, including the establishment of e-petitions and the setting up of the Backbench Business Committee (see Table 7.1).

In 2005, he was a leading member of the group of dissident Labour MPs who voted against Tony Blair's proposal to allow terrorist suspects to be held for 90 days without trial. This resulted in Blair's perhaps most important Commons defeat.

In his own constituency in Nottingham, he leads an initiative for early intervention (the Teenage Pregnancy Taskforce) to reduce teenage pregnancy, another of his political concerns. He presses for greater government action on teenage pregnancy.

Zac Goldsmith – Conservative – Richmond Park and North Kingston

A new MP in 2010, Goldsmith is a tireless environmental campaigner. It is often said that his great personal wealth enables him to be independent, but this does not detract from his determination. He has pressed the new coalition government on two major issues. One concerns the proposed changes to the local planning laws (passing through Parliament in 2011–12), which should ensure both local involvement in planning decisions and assurances that the environment is protected in planning decisions. His championing of environmentally friendly planning safeguards runs counter to the policies of several government departments that are only concerned with economic growth. The other issue concerns harmful emissions: the government should put pressure on the European Union to introduce ambitious targets for control of these emissions.

His independence is indicated by his extensive use of questions to ministers and Early Day Motions, when backbenchers may draw attention to issues that concern them. One of his prominent local campaigns is his Support our Small Shops campaign in Richmond, Barnes and Kingston in South-West London.

Tom Watson – Labour – West Bromwich East

Watson was a junior minister up to 2006 when, in a blaze of publicity, he resigned his post, asserting that Tony Blair should resign as prime minister, largely over what he saw as his failed campaign in Iraq.

But it was in 2010 that he became well known for his campaign to publicise the widespread use of phone hacking by journalists, especially at the *News of the World*. As a member of the House of Commons Culture, Media and Sport Select Committee, he relentlessly pursued News International and the Murdoch family (who are major shareholders) over their part in the phone hacking scandal. His campaign led to the establishment of the Leveson judicial inquiry into the behaviour of journalists as well as the relationships between the press, politicians and senior police officers. He was joined in this venture by Louise Mensch (Conservative – Corby), a flamboyant, independent-minded new MP. This was therefore a good example of cross-party cooperation. Mensch has also called for the shutting down of social networks during any repeat of the inner city riots of the summer of 2011.

Steve Rotheram – Labour – Liverpool Walton

A former mayor of Liverpool, Rotheram is an example of how a backbench MP can use the new digital media to mount a successful campaign. In 1989, 96 football fans (mostly from Liverpool) were crushed to death at Hillsborough (Sheffield Wednesday's ground) at the start of an FA Cup semi-final when one end of the ground became overcrowded. Since then, Rotheram and many others have campaigned for all the evidence and documentation concerning the incident to be made public. Their contention is that a good deal of the truth about police actions had been concealed.

He sponsored an e-petition, which obtained 140,000 signatures, thus triggering a House of Commons debate. The debate ended with a unanimous vote for full disclosure. As a result of his and others' actions, the government agreed to release all papers about the disaster, including cabinet discussions.

Priti Patel – Conservative – Witham

Patel is on the right wing of the Conservative Party. A new MP in 2010, she has quickly made it clear that she does not support the government's position on Europe. She now leads a campaign to fight against closer political integration in the EU and for a new referendum in Britain to bring back sovereignty from the EU to the UK. She is a leading member of Conservative Home, a faction that campaigns for a return to basic conservative values and which opposes concessions to the Liberal Democrats which have pushed the government to a more liberal position. She is thus proving to be a thorn in the government's side by stirring up traditional Conservative opinion against coalition politics.

Examples of backbench success

If we are to suggest that backbench influence is growing, we need further evidence. This can be provided by examples of successes enjoyed by MPs against government official policy. These have included:

- **Tuition fees.** Though there was extensive backbench opposition (especially among Liberal Democrats) to the raising of the maximum university tuition fees to £9,000 per annum in 2010, a number of concessions were obtained from the government under the threat of a major revolt. In particular, the legislation included a commitment that universities charging the maximum would have to admit a quota of young people from deprived backgrounds.

- **The privatisation of forests.** In 2010, it was proposed that many thousands of acres of forest should be sold off to private landowners. There was widespread opposition and a group of Conservative and Liberal Democrat MPs, mostly representing rural constituencies, joined with the Labour opposition to urge a rethink. The government abandoned the plan before it went to a vote in the Commons, which the government would surely have lost.

- **The NHS reform.** While the Health and Social Care Bill was passing through the Commons in the summer of 2011, widespread concern was expressed among MPs, notably Liberal Democrats. The government was forced to compromise by these dissident MPs, admitting hospital doctors and nurses into the new health service commissioning groups. Interestingly this sparked a counter-rebellion among Conservative backbenchers who opposed the compromise. This was fought out in the committee stage of the bill (normally a formality), after which the concessions remained. This was an unusual example of an issue being fought out on the backbenches rather than in cabinet.

- **The planning reform.** The government's proposals to simplify and reform the laws on local planning are being debated during the winter of 2011–12. These have already proved to be controversial and many MPs are pressing for compromises. The main issue is a belief that the new regulations will mean that economic considerations in planning decisions will be more important than environmental considerations. In other words, large areas of the countryside and greenfield land may be placed under threat. MPs who are concerned with the quality of rural life (such as Zac Goldsmith) will press for changes to the legislation. These MPs have already been successful in bringing these matters to public and media attention.

The counter-arguments

So far, we have only considered the evidence suggesting that backbench MPs have become more influential than in recent history. There is, however, a good deal of evidence that MPs remain relatively unimportant. This includes the following:

- Despite great pressures, the coalition government has survived. This is the case even with many predictions that it could not last long. In some senses, the coalition's fragility is its strength. When backbench Liberal Democrats (and occasionally right-wing Conservatives) have threatened the coalition with a revolt, there was always the prospect that the government would lose a key vote and fall from power. This would mean a fresh election and the possibility that many backbench MPs might lose their seats. Liberal Democrats in particular are constrained by the collapse in the party's opinion poll fortunes. In other words, for many, the need to preserve the coalition takes precedence over their personal political beliefs.
- The coalition has not yet lost an important vote. While it has withdrawn some proposals (such as privatisation of forests) before legislation, it has not been thwarted on any major policy. While there was widespread public opposition to raising tuition fees and to NHS reform, backbench MPs remained reluctant to reflect this in their voting in the House.
- The Nottingham University data (shown above) look compelling, but many of the revolts mentioned have been very small. There have been no major backbench dissident movements as yet.
- The fundamental factors behind backbench weakness still remain. The prime minister still has powers of patronage, which demands loyalty. Nick Clegg has similar control over his party. Few MPs want to precipitate a general election by defeating the government. The whips still have plenty of ammunition in their battle to maintain party unity.

Summary

Has backbench influence returned? Is this a new age of the effective backbench MP? It is, perhaps, a little early to answer this question. It is certainly safe to say that we are seeing greater activism and independence among backbenchers. It is also true that coalition government is a 'game changer'. However, this is not yet a 'golden age' for backbenchers in the nineteenth-century sense of the word. The recent House of Commons reforms and the growing importance of e-democracy may well give backbenchers more opportunities to exert influence, but the question is: will they take advantage of these new opportunities?

The key points in this chapter have been:

- Coalition should, in theory, give more influence to backbench MPs.
- There is a good deal of evidence to suggest backbench MPs have become more active and independent.
- Despite party loyalty, we can identify a number of backbench MPs who have influence and have been able to change government policy.
- Nevertheless, the fundamental relationship between government and Parliament has not really changed, despite coalition.
- The coalition government has suffered no major defeats.

Exam focus

To consolidate your knowledge of this chapter, answer the following questions:

1 To what extent can MPs influence government?
2 Explain why government exercises so much control over the House of Commons.
3 How has coalition government affected the relationship between government and Parliament?
4 Distinguish between frontbench and backbench MPs.

Chapter 8

Lords reform: what next?

Exam success

The up-to-date facts, examples and arguments in this chapter will help you to produce good-quality answers in your AS unit tests in the following areas of the specification:

Edexcel	AQA	OCR
Unit 2	Unit 2	Unit F852
Parliament	Parliament	The legislature
	The British Constitution	

Context

May 2011 saw the publication of the much anticipated House of Lords Reform Draft Bill. Long in gestation, this bill represented the first concerted effort on the part of the government to resolve the impasse over the second stage of House of Lords reform since the proposals contained in the 2007 white paper ran aground in the Lords. While the 2011 proposals contained little that was genuinely new, there was at least a degree of cross-party consensus over precisely how the process of Lords reform, started back in 1999 with the House of Lords Act, might be taken through to its natural conclusion.

This chapter considers the provision of the 2011 draft bill against the backdrop of efforts to reform the Lords over the course of the past 12 years. In so doing, it answers the following questions:

- What was proposed in the 2011 House of Lords Reform Draft Bill?
- Why has the second stage of Lords reform proven so problematic?
- How likely is it that the new draft bill will pass into law?

What was proposed in the 2011 House of Lords Reform Draft Bill?

Anyone approaching the topic of Lords reform for the first time in 2011, oblivious to all that had gone before, could have been forgiven for seeing genuine promise in the proposals contained in the draft bill published in May of that year (see Table 8.1, right column).

Table 8.1 2007 white paper and 2011 Draft Reform Bill compared

2007 white paper	2011 House of Lords Reform Draft Bill
The Commons' primacy to be maintained	The Commons' primacy to be maintained
A reduced chamber of 540 members	A second chamber of 300 members
A 50:50 split between elected and appointed Lords	An 80:20 split between elected and appointed Lords

A single, long, non-renewable term of office	A single, non-renewable term of 15 years for Lords
Appointed peers to be selected by a new, independent Statutory Appointments Commission	60 appointed peers to be chosen by an independent Statutory Appointments Commission
Elected peers to be chosen under a partially open regional party list system	240 elected Lords to be chosen under STV (or an open list system)
A system of staggered elections, similar to that in the US Senate, with one third of elected members being chosen at each election	A system of staggered elections, similar to that in the US Senate, with one third of elected members (i.e. 80) being chosen at each election
Elections to coincide with elections to the European Parliament, i.e. every 5 years	Elections to coincide with elections to the Commons, i.e. every 5 years
20% of Lords to be non-party political appointees and no party to have an overall majority in the chamber	The expectation that appointed members would bring a non-party-political perspective to the work carried out by the reformed House of Lords

Source: adapted from *The House of Lords: Reform White Paper* (CM 7027), February 2007, and the *House of Lords Reform Draft Bill* (CM 8077), May 2011.

The proposals set out in that bill offered the prospect of a fundamental shake-up for the second chamber that would see a halving of its membership as well as a move from a house of political placemen, the 'Great and the Good' and former hereditaries, towards a legislative chamber in which 80% of members would be chosen under a proportional electoral system.

Those more familiar with the meandering and tortuous course of Lords reform since 1999, however, might have viewed the proposals in a different light.

- At the time of the 1997 general election, New Labour had offered the promise of a reformed chamber more socially representative of the broader population.
- Though the single explicit promise in that party's 1997 manifesto was a commitment to remove the right of the 759 hereditary peers to sit and vote in the chamber, the expectation was that this would be no more than a modest first step towards a fully reformed chamber.
- The much heralded 'second stage' of Lords reform failed to materialise (see Box 8.1).

Box 8.1   Max Hastings' verdict on Lords reform (2006)

[...] nothing [was to] become more symbolic of the Blair government's failure than the fate of its flagship constitutional reform. Nine years down the track, the Lords [was] still stuck in a siding, after half-baked changes that settled nothing. As with so much else this government has attempted, the purpose has been admirable, the execution lamentable.

Source: Hastings, M. (2006) 'A second chamber of time-servers and losers would be contemptible', *Guardian*, 23 October.

The House of Lords Act (1999)

New Labour's first, and ultimately final, step along the road of Lords reform was the removal of all but 92 hereditary peers under the House of Lords Act (1999), the party's original intention to remove the voting rights of all hereditaries having been watered down as a result of an amendment that secured safe passage of the reform bill through the upper house.

Despite clear manifesto pledges to reform the Lords further at both the 2001 and 2005 general elections, the closest the party came to completing reform of the chamber came with the votes in the Commons and the Lords (see Table 8.2) that effectively ended any prospect of the model set out in the 2007 White Paper (see Table 8.1, left column) being adopted.

Table 8.2 Parliamentary votes on Lords reform, March 2007

Option	House of Commons			House of Lords		
	Yes	No	Maj.	Yes	No	Maj.
Abolition	163	416	−253	No vote taken		
100% appointed	196	375	−179	361	121	+240
50% elected	155	418	−263	46	410	−364
60% elected	178	392	−214	45	393	−348
80% elected	305	267	+38	114	336	−222
100% elected	337	224	+113	122	326	−204

Source: adapted from Russell, M. (2007) 'The House of Lords — reform past and present', *Politics Review*, Vol. 17, No. 1, September.

Why has the second stage of Lords reform proven so problematic?

It is possible to identify a number of reasons that may explain why the second stage of Lords reform has proven so difficult to execute.

The status of the Commons

- The desire to preserve the primacy of the Commons, not least in the minds of MPs themselves, has proven a significant barrier to reform.
- The Lords' status as a lesser 'revising chamber' in a system of asymmetrical bicameralism has long been justified by the fact that the second chamber is unelected, thereby lacking its own electoral mandate.
- Any move towards an elected or partially elected chamber would strike at the heart of this assumption, while at the same time bringing into question the practice of drawing the prime minister, along with the bulk of his or her cabinet colleagues, from the Commons.

Resistance in the Lords

- Any reform bill would necessarily require the support of peers themselves in order to pass onto the statute books.
- It is unlikely, however, that there would be majority support in the Lords for any measure that would immediately remove most incumbent peers from

political office — that would be akin to the proverbial 'turkeys voting for Christmas'.

- The measure could, of course, be forced through the Lords using the Parliament Act. However, there is a question mark over whether that act can legitimately be used to force through a significant reshaping of the upper chamber.

The performance of the part-reformed Lords

- There has been a general agreement that the part-reformed chamber has worked with a degree of efficiency in its primary function, that of scrutinising the work of the elected Commons.
- Though the concept of an unelected chamber may appear to challenge twenty-first-century sensibilities, therefore, there is a sense that 'if it ain't broke, don't try to fix it'.
- There is a danger that an elected second chamber might simply end up echoing the first or that its members (currently free from the need to pander to voters) would lose their independence once their political futures depended upon maintaining electoral support.

A lack of consensus

- There has been no real consensus as to how to proceed.
- Some favour an entirely elected second chamber, others prefer to stick with the current model of appointments, with a full spectrum of partially elected models strung out at equidistant intervals between these two polar extremes.

How likely is it that the new draft bill will pass into law?

Back in 2007, in the wake of the Commons' ballot that saw more than half of MPs vote in favour of an elected chamber, Jack Straw offered his thoughts on what might happen once the proposal had passed through to the 'Other Place'. 'I don't know what the bookies are offering,' he remarked, 'but the odds will be very short on the peers backing an all-appointed chamber, and long on any alternative.' He was, of course, entirely correct in his analysis.

Is progress any more likely today than it was 5 years ago?
The proposal
On the face of it, what was proposed in 2011 is an almost perfect facsimile of what was set out back in 2007 (see Table 8.1). One might conclude, therefore, that the bill is likely to face precisely the same fate as that White Paper. Though the idea of single-term, staggered elections and a different electoral system from that used in elections to the Commons addresses some of the concerns raised above, these provisions appeared almost verbatim in the abandoned 2007 white paper.

The Lords in question

The proposals themselves are not the only factor in play when seeking to gauge the bill's chances of success. One must also look at the composition and performance of the current chamber (i.e. consider the *need* for change, as opposed to focusing entirely on the *substance* of that change).

In terms of performance, the Lords remains an effective check on the power of the Commons and, by implication, on the government of the day:

- In the 2010–11 session, the Lords defeated the government on 14 separate occasions.
- At the time of writing, the figure for the 2011–12 session stood at 23 separate defeats.

In terms of composition, however, some have questioned the way in which the membership of the Lords has evolved since those 2007 votes:

- First, there has been a significant increase in the numbers of peers entitled to sit in the Lords, raising issues of efficiency and attendance.
- Second, though peers are commonly said to bring a wealth of experience to their deliberations, the primary professional background of peers has grown increasingly narrow (see Table 8.3). This raises the question of whether the second chamber can continue to be the effective revising chamber that it once was.

Table 8.3 Declared primary professional backgrounds of peers

	Area	Number	% of Lords
1.	Representative politics	151	22%
2.	Business and commerce	61	9%
3.	Banking and finance	59	8%
4.	Higher education	59	8%
5.	Legal professions	54	8%
6.	Clergy or religious	29	4%
7.	Journalism, media and publishing	25	4%
8.	Voluntary sector, NGOs and think tanks	25	4%
9.	Other private sector	23	3%
10.	Trade unions	21	3%
11.	Agriculture and horticulture	20	3%
12.	International affairs and diplomacy	18	3%
13.	Medical and healthcare	15	2%
14.	Political staff and activists	15	2%
15.	Culture, arts and sport	14	2%
16.	Armed forces	12	2%
17.	Other public sector	12	2%
18.	Civil service (UK)	10	1%
19.	Police	8	1%
20.	Local authority administration	8	1%
21.	Architecture, engineering and construction	5	1%
22.	Education and training (not HE)	5	1%

23.	Transport	5	1%
24.	Royal family staff	2	0%
25.	Manual and skilled trades	1	0%
	Unclassified	42	6%
	Total included	699	100%

Source: Russell, M. and Benton, M. (2010), *Analysis of Existing Data on the Breadth of Expertise and Experience in the House of Lords*, The Constitution Unit.

Should the UK retain an unelected second chamber?

YES

- Unelected peers have a wealth of life experience that may be lost if the UK moves towards an elected or partially elected second chamber.
- Freedom from elections allows for weaker party control in the Lords and enhanced independence for its members.
- An elected Lords could undermine the primacy of the Commons.
- The Parliament Acts of 1911 and 1949 (and the Salisbury Doctrine) prevent the unelected chamber from indefinitely frustrating the ambitions of the Commons.

NO

- It is wrong in principle for voters to be denied the opportunity to hold legislators accountable through the ballot box.
- An elected or partially elected chamber would have greater legitimacy, allowing it to scrutinise the work of the Commons from a position of greater authority.
- The unelected Lords is not socially representative of the UK population at large.
- The Lords has used its legislative powers to frustrate the ambitions of elected politicians.

Summary

- Though the 2011 House of Lords Reform Draft Bill was well received, it goes no further than the 2007 white paper that ran aground in the Lords 5 years ago.
- The promise of single, 15-year fixed terms for Lords, staggered elections and a proportional system addresses some of the problems arising from the creation of a second elected legislative chamber.
- Changes in the composition of the Lords since 2007 have strengthened the case for reform.
- It remains unlikely that the proposals in the current form will clear the Lords without significant amendment.

Exam focus

To consolidate your knowledge of this chapter, answer the following questions:

1 How did the 2011 House of Lords Reform Draft Bill differ from the 2007 White Paper?
2 How significant were the changes brought about by the 1999 House of Lords Act?
3 Why has it been so difficult to achieve the second stage of Lords reform?
4 Why has there been resistance to a wholly elected second chamber?
5 'If it ain't broke, don't try to fix it.' To what extent do you agree with this view of Lords reform?

Chapter 9

A new UK Bill of Rights: a pointless exercise?

Exam success

The up-to-date facts, examples and arguments in this chapter will help you to produce good-quality answers in your AS unit tests in the following areas of the specification:

Edexcel	AQA	OCR
Unit 2	**Unit 2**	**Unit F852**
Judges and civil liberties	The British Constitution	The judiciary

Context

August 2011 saw the publication of the discussion paper 'Do we need a UK Bill of Rights?' by the Commission on a Bill of Rights established by the Liberal–Conservative coalition back in March. The creation of this commission and the start of a 'national conversation' on rights represented the coalition's first tentative steps towards dealing with what has become an increasingly controversial issue since the 1998 Human Rights Act came into force back in October 2000.

This chapter considers the merits of this consultation exercise in the context both of perceptions of the Human Rights Act and the difficulties that will inevitably accompany any attempt to tackle its supposed shortcomings through the creation of a new rights model for the UK. In so doing, it answers the following questions:

- What is the coalition proposing?
- Why is legislating for rights inherently problematic in the UK context?
- Is the entire exercise essentially pointless?

What is the coalition proposing?

The 2011 discussion paper

Unsurprisingly, the commission's discussion paper did little more than 'get the ball rolling'. Coming in at just 11 well-spaced pages (excluding contact details and endnotes), its limitations were readily apparent:

- The questions if offered for public consultation were overly generalised (see Box 9.1).
- Its anticipated reporting date (by the end of 2012) suggested that legislation would not follow ahead of the next general election.
- The document consists almost entirely of background material that (a) is already widely available and discussed, and (b) does little to help the

general reader (i.e. the broader public) to address the subtleties inherent in the questions posed.

Box 9.1 Questions for public consultation

1 Do you think we need a UK Bill of Rights?
2 If so, what do you think a UK Bill of Rights should contain?
3 How do you think it should apply to the UK as a whole, including its four component countries of England, Northern Ireland, Scotland and Wales?
4 Having regard to our terms of reference, are there any other views which you would like to put forward at this stage?

Source: Commission on a Bill of Rights (2011), 'Do we need a UK Bill of Rights?'

Party positions

Conservatives

- From the beginning of his time as party leader, David Cameron offered a root-and-branch approach to tackling perceived deficiencies in the Human Rights Act (HRA).
- Though initially suggesting that a Conservative government would 'reform, replace or scrap' the HRA, the party's position became far clearer in 2006 (see Box 9.2).
- Since that point, the Conservatives have been committed to replacing, as opposed to amending or developing, the existing HRA.

Box 9.2 Cameron on the HRA (2006)

We need a new approach because:

- the Human Rights Act has made it harder to protect our security
- it is hampering our fight against crime and terrorism
- it has done little to protect our liberties
- it has helped create rights without responsibilities

Labour

- As the party that introduced the HRA, Labour has been disinclined to criticise it publicly.
- The party's preference has been to fine-tune the act and provide additional guidance for those engaged in the administration of justice.
- This approach implies that there had been a failure to 'apply' the HRA effectively on the part of judges — as opposed to more fundamental flaws in the legislation itself.

Liberal Democrats

- The Lib Dems have looked to 'extend' rather than 'limit' the scope of the HRA.

These general positions were reflected in the parties' 2010 general election manifestos (see Table 9.1).

Table 9.1 Manifestos compared on the HRA, 2010

Conservative	Labour	Liberal Democrat
To protect our freedoms from state encroachment and encourage greater social responsibility, we will replace the Human Rights Act with a UK Bill of Rights.	We are proud to have brought in the Human Rights Act, enabling British citizens to take action in British courts rather than having to wait years to seek redress in Strasbourg. We will not repeal it or resile from it.	We will ensure that everyone has the same protections under the law by protecting the Human Rights Act.

The coalition agreement and the HRA

Successful coalitions are characterised by compromise and the Liberal–Conservative approach to bridging the gap between each party's manifesto positions on the HRA is a case in point. While the section of the coalition agreement that dealt with civil liberties contained a number of concrete proposals (for example, the scrapping of Labour's ID card scheme), the gulf between the two parties on the question of the HRA was bridged by means of a single sentence that appeared ideally suited to the task of 'kicking' a potentially divisive issue 'into the long grass' (see Table 9.2).

Table 9.2 The coalition agreement on the issue of civil liberties

Firm commitments	General policies and intentions
Civil liberties	**Civil liberties**
■ The proposed ID card scheme to be scrapped	■ Strengthening the Freedom of Information Act
■ The DNA records of suspected persons to be kept for a shorter period of time	■ **A Commission to review the European Convention on Human Rights to establish whether a new British version can be adopted**
■ A Freedom Bill to be passed, though its terms are to be determined	■ Review of anti-terrorism legislation
	■ Greater regulation of the use of CCTV
	■ To reduce controls on non-violent protest

Source: Fairclough, P., McNaughton, N. and Magee, E. (2011) *Annual Survey 2011,* Philip Allan Updates.

Why is legislating for rights inherently problematic in the UK context?

The way in which rights have traditionally been protected in the UK

■ The rights available to UK citizens have traditionally been based on legal principles, as opposed to the kinds of explicit guarantees commonly referred to a 'positive rights' (see Box 9.3). The concept of a UK Bill of Rights would therefore represent a dramatic shift in political and judicial culture.

The basis of rights in the UK

- There are no British rights that are 'fundamental' in the sense that they enjoy special constitutional protection against Parliament. The liberties of the subject are implications derived from two principles:

  The first principle is that we may say or do as we please, provided that we do not transgress the substantive law or the legal rights of others.

  The second principle is that the Crown and public authorities may only act if they have the power to do so.

- These powers can derive from legislation, common law and — as far as the Crown is concerned — the royal prerogative.

- Our laws are a combination of statute law and the principles of the common law and equity developed by our courts.

- Our system is based upon the constitutional principles of Parliamentary sovereignty and the Rule of Law.

Source: Commission on a Bill of Rights (2011), 'Do We Need a UK Bill of Rights?'

The absence of a codified constitution

- The presence of a codified constitution generally offers a degree of entrenchment to those rights which its authors choose to guarantee.

- In the UK, however, parliamentary sovereignty and the primacy of statute law create a situation in which any attempt to legislate for rights would not protect any rights identified from subsequent encroachment.

- Though David Cameron has previously argued that a degree of entrenchment could be provided by adding a UK Bill of Rights to the list of measures that the Commons cannot force through the Lords by means of the Parliament Acts, this would be a poor substitute for a UK Bill of Rights properly entrenched within a codified constitution.

The UK's commitments under the European Convention on Human Rights (ECHR)

- The Human Rights Act (1998) did little more than incorporate the main provision of the ECHR (to which the UK has long been a signatory) into UK law.

- This meant that individuals could pursue cases relating to Convention rights through the UK courts, as opposed to having to take their quarrel to the European Court of Human Rights (ECtHR) at Strasbourg.

- Repealing the HRA, limiting its scope or replacing it with a UK model would do nothing to remove our commitments under the ECHR, as Marcel Berlins noted in the *Guardian* back in 2006 (see Box 9.4).

- The ECHR originated at the Council of Europe, as opposed to the EEC or the EU. However, while the UK could in theory withdraw from the Convention, it has become a *de facto* requirement of EU membership — all 27 EU member states are signatories to it.

Is the entire exercise essentially pointless?

There are basically two arguments in favour of the view that the exercise being undertaken by the Liberal–Conservative coalition is essentially pointless.

The UK does not need a Bill of Rights
- The kinds of rights that would be guaranteed in a bill of rights have long been enshrined in common law and/or parliamentary statute.
- In the absence of an entrenched codified constitution, the Human Rights Act does as much as can be done under UK law.

There is little prospect of success
- There is no consensus within the coalition regarding the way forward.
- There is a lack of consensus beyond the coalition regarding precisely what should be included in such a Bill of Rights and what should be left out.
- The terms of reference of the Commission on a Bill of Rights and its opening discussion paper offer little prospect of any legislation in this area ahead of the next general election.
- No matter what happens in respect of the HRA, the UK will continue to be bound by the terms of the ECHR.

Should the UK replace the HRA with a new bill of rights?
YES
- The HRA has placed too much power into the hands of senior judges, thus challenging the doctrine of parliamentary sovereignty.
- A UK Bill of Rights would protect rights in a manner more in keeping with our traditions.
- The HRA is widely ridiculed in the press and has lost the confidence of the broader public.

NO
- Guaranteeing certain rights in this way would serve only to undermine others not formally enshrined.
- Repeal of the HRA would not remove the UK's obligations under the ECHR.
- In the absence of a codified constitution, there is no way of effectively entrenching any new bill of rights.

Summary

- Codified and universal guarantees of rights and freedoms inevitably give rise to public controversy, while at the same time empowering the judiciary. This is true of the HRA and would also apply to any British bill of rights.
- The UK would find it difficult to withdraw from the ECHR. Replacing the HRA would therefore do little more than force citizens to take their cases to Strasbourg once more.
- The absence of a codified constitution makes it difficult to offer a UK Bill of Rights any degree of entrenchment.
- There is no consensus regarding the way forward.
- The discussion paper of the Commission on a Bill of Rights offers little prospect of concrete change. It appears more suited to papering over divisions within the coalition on this issue than bringing about genuine change.

Exam focus

To consolidate your knowledge of this chapter, answer the following questions:

1 Present the case for a UK Bill of Rights.
2 Present the case against a UK Bill of Rights.
3 Why, in the UK context, is it difficult to legislate on rights?
4 To what extent do you agree with the view that 'the entire exercise is essentially pointless'?

Chapter 10

Briefings

This chapter will bring you up to date with some of the most recent political developments and demonstrate how they are relevant to your studies in government and politics.

The Fox affair: individual ministerial responsibility and private advisers

The facts

Liam Fox was appointed defence secretary by David Cameron in his first coalition government. It was, however, revealed that a personal friend of Dr Fox, Adam Werritty, had been present during several foreign visits made by Fox, including a number of sensitive meetings in the Middle East. Mr Werritty passed himself off as a political adviser to Dr Fox, but, in fact, was not registered as a political adviser and Fox himself denied that he was. Questions were asked about why Werritty was allowed at these meetings, whether he had access to sensitive defence information and who was financing his travel and accommodation. It was ultimately revealed that Werritty was being financed by a number of wealthy businessmen who had links with the USA and Israel. Fox denied that Werritty had access to sensitive information.

Initially Fox denied any wrong-doing, but an inquiry conducted by Gus O'Donnell, the cabinet secretary (Britain's most senior civil servant), revealed that Werritty's connections with Dr Fox had broken the Ministerial Code that does not allow such personal friends to be too closely associated with ministers on official business. Liam Fox resigned on 14 October 2011. He accepted that he had made serious 'misjudgements', though he denied that there had been anything sinister or corrupt about his association with Adam Werritty.

The political significance of the Fox affair

This affair does not reflect on the government or David Cameron. It appears that Dr Fox had brought the problem on himself and had acted independently in this matter. However, Fox was a leader of the Conservative right-wing tendency and this means that his faction has lost some representation in the cabinet. David Cameron himself may well feel uneasy that such a prominent right winger is now on the backbenches and is no longer bound by the discipline of collective ministerial responsibility. In other words, Liam Fox may prove to be a thorn in Cameron's side, especially over British relations with Europe.

Chapter 10

Relating the affair to the study of government and politics

The Fox case illustrates a number of issues:

- It is a very good example of the doctrine of individual ministerial responsibility (IMR) at work. There are three main situations where IMR applies and ministers may resign:
  1 when a government department makes a serious error, the minister in charge may have to accept responsibility
  2 over a minister's personal conduct (i.e. a 'scandal')
  3 over an error of judgement by a minister
  The Fox case is an example of the third type.
- It highlights the importance of private advisers. The use of such advisers has grown so much over the past 20 years that their activities have to be regulated. In this case, Werritty was not regulated so he and his friend, the minister, had to go. Private advisers have to be registered as official parts of the governing process.
- Cameron replaced Fox with Philip Hammond, the transport secretary. Hammond is seen as a loyalist and a 'safe pair of hands'. Cameron has therefore used his patronage power to move the balance of the cabinet more to the centre of Conservative politics.

The Commons vote on a Europe referendum: digital democracy reveals a split in the Conservative Party

The facts

As part of the spread of digital democracy, it is now established that if at least 100,000 people give their name to an e-petition on an important political issue, requesting a parliamentary debate, Parliament may make time for such a debate. 140,000 people thus called for a parliamentary debate on the question of whether a referendum should be held on whether Britain should remain in the European Union.

The debate was scheduled for 24 October 2011. There was no doubt that the result of the debate would be to reject a referendum on EU membership, not least because both Labour and the Liberal Democrats would vote against it. The real question was: how many Conservatives would support the demand for a referendum? David Cameron gambled by issuing a three-line whip to his MPs (i.e. a compulsory instruction to support the government), requiring them to reject the call for the referendum. It was a gamble because this tactic might reveal the strength of Euro-sceptic feeling in the Conservative Party.

In the event, 81 Conservatives disobeyed the whip and voted in favour of a referendum, while approximately 30 abstained. This represented a surprisingly big revolt against the authority of David Cameron.

The political significance of the referendum vote

The main issue thrown up by this vote is the extent to which there is a section of the Conservative Party that is seriously concerned about Britain's relationship with the European Union, many of whom support the idea that Britain might leave the EU altogether. The vote indicated two things: first that this Conservative faction is larger than was previously thought, possibly representing half the parliamentary party; second that their strength of feeling must be quite high as they were willing to defy a three-line party whip.

John Major's time in office, from 1990 to 1997, was dogged by constant problems with the Euro-sceptic wing of the party and David Cameron may be about to experience similar problems.

Relating this event to the study of government and politics

The EU referendum vote illustrates a number of issues:

- It highlights the potential of digital democracy. The e-petition resulted in a parliamentary debate which has had major repercussions. If parliamentary debates, triggered by e-petitions, become more common, they may become a major feature of democracy in the UK. Without the petition, this issue would not have been debated in the Commons because the government has a great deal of control over the parliamentary agenda.
- The size of the Conservative 'revolt' demonstrates how divided the Conservative Party remains on the issue of Britain's relationship with the EU.
- It may be that the Conservative Euro-sceptic faction will force the government into renegotiating the terms of British membership in the future, probably involving some opt-outs from parts of the EU treaties.
- As the Liberal Democrats remain very pro-EU, the issue may well cause stress within the coalition.

The Occupy London movement grows: the influence of new social movements

The facts

The Occupy London movement is part of a worldwide campaign that involves the occupation of parts of the centres of major cities by protesters. The movement contains a mixture of different political traditions, including socialism, anarchism, environmentalism and spiritualism. The broad thrust of the campaign is anti-capitalism in the light of the current economic crisis, together with opposition to what is seen as 'corporate greed', demonstrated by excessive salaries in finance and business, unjustified bonuses and tax-avoidance schemes. It therefore has both moral and political aspects.

The London branch of this movement has pitched camps in both Paternoster Square in front of St Paul's Cathedral and Finsbury Square. Both locations are close to centres of banking and business in the capital. Similar camps can be found in New York, Madrid and several other major cities. By November 2011, the authorities at St Paul's Cathedral had decided to have the protesters removed, but a split among the senior clerics led to a postponement of such action.

The political significance of this movement

As yet it is too early to estimate the influence of this movement, both in the UK and internationally. Certainly it caused something of a crisis in the upper circles of the Church of England. It forced many senior members of the Church to reconsider their attitude to modern capitalism and its perceived 'excesses'. The Church of England does not have great political influence today, but it would be a fairly significant development if it declared itself 'officially' part of the broad political movement that hopes to see significant regulations introduced to curb corporate 'greed and irresponsibility'.

Relating this movement to the study of government and politics

There is nothing very new about Occupy London and its umbrella movement, Indignant. All international conferences have been marked by major demonstrations by a similar coalition of protest movements. However, it once again highlights how pressure-group politics is changing. The following conclusions can be drawn:

- The movement was pulled together very rapidly and in a coordinated way. This demonstrates the importance of social networking and digital communications in group politics. It is now possible to rally huge groups of people quickly and effectively at short notice.
- The movement can be seen, to some extent, as a reaction to a perceived 'failure' of conventional politics. In particular, traditional forms of representation — especially Parliament and the parties — are seen to be failing to reflect popular concerns. This kind of direct action is growing because of such failures. Even traditional pressure groups are now being marginalised in favour of direct action.
- If democracy is about dispersing power and influence widely, and if it is about active popular participation, such movements as Occupy London *enhance* modern democracy.
- If, on the other hand, these movements give an impression of wide public support because of the publicity they attract, when, in fact, they are not a reflection of wider opinion, they *distort* democracy.

In the end, what still matters is which parties win elections and gain power. New social movements have influence but no power.